STEEPLE PEOPLE

A Collection of Humorous and Inspiring Stories

by Steve Davis

VA

Vabella Publishing

Vabella Publishing
P.O. Box 1052
Carrollton, Georgia 30112
www.vabella.com

Cover design by Sarah Dockery - Sudoc Designs: www.sudocdesigns.com

Cover photograph "abandoned" by Dave Huss / www.istockphoto.com

Manufactured in the United States of America

Library of Congress Control Number: 2006924355

10-digit ISBN 0-9712204-3-3

13-digit ISBN 978-0-9712204-3-0

To Sheri, Tyler, Natalie, and D.D.

Contents

Chapter One: Church

Chapter Two: Christian Living

Preface

When I began serving First Baptist Church, Carrollton, Georgia, as pastor in the fall of 1995, I was told that one expectation of the pastor was a weekly newsletter article. And so I began writing. I have never thought of myself as a writer, but I found some joy in the process and got enough kudos to keep at it. Over the years, countless people have said they enjoyed my articles, and many have inquired if I would ever put them in a book. These same people I am now counting on to purchase one (or several) books in order to make this a profitable proposition.

I want to say thanks to the congregation of First Baptist for their support and for providing much of the inspiration for the book. You are the "Steeple People" who have defined church for me and who have blessed my life immensely. And by the way, the names of church members and friends have not been changed so that they might be thoroughly embarrassed or enjoy, perhaps, their "fifteen minutes of fame." For those outside of Carrollton, Georgia, who might stumble upon a copy of this book, remember that these articles were written for a church newsletter from 1995-2005 and thus capture a moment in time and also contain references to local establishments. To the wonderful staff at the church, I could never thank you enough. Specifically, thanks to Susan Mashburn for her painstaking work in putting the newsletter together every week and in the process, typing, editing and sometimes improving my articles. And a special thanks goes to Amanda Redman, Sonja Bagby, and Melissa Dobbs for the compilation, working and reworking of the final form of these articles and to John Bell, friend and author, for his advice on the book-making process.

To my family, Sheri, Tyler and Natalie, you are the inspiration for my life and for many of my stories. I love you and I thank you for your constant support.

CHURCH

Church

Steeple People

We sure began Sunday with a bang! In case you haven't heard, our steeple was hit by lightning during the weekend storms. Does it surprise you that lightning hit our steeple? Not me. Churches are not immune from the forces of nature or evil in the world. Churches and Christians take direct hits all the time. However, I've been thinking about our steeple in an entirely different way. Steeples attract people as well as lightning— and for the same reason. Our steeple is the highest point around, rising above the Carrollton landscape and pointing its finger to the heavens. Thus, it attracts lightning. People too. People wander into our church all the time because they saw the steeple. What kind of people? Hungry. Happy. Homeless. Limping. Skipping. Lonely. Angry. Depressed. Bewildered. Disappointed. In the words of Charles Poole: "People come to the steeples because they assume that wherever there is a steeple at the top there is a sanctuary at the bottom." [1]People come—for healing, rest and a chance to start over. People are nourished in the sanctuary by the friends they see, hymns they sing and sermons they hear. Lightning may have damaged our steeple, but it can't deter our church. Real church takes place beneath the steeple.

---

[1] Charles E. Poole, *Don't Cry Past Tuesday* (Smyth & Helwys, 1991) 8.

What Would the Colonel Say?
There is a new combination restaurant in our community. Kentucky Fried Chicken (KFC) and Taco Bell are combined in one restaurant. No kidding! The Colonel would roll over in … It looks like the kind of place Sheri and I should like. She grew up in Houston, Texas, and loves Mexican food. I grew up in LA (Lower Alabama), and every Southern boy loves KFC. We haven't been inside the restaurant yet, but my imagination is running wild. Do they serve tacos and a drumstick? Yuck! Enchiladas and potato salad? Yuck! Fajitas and cole slaw? Yuck! Well, you get the picture. Some things don't seem to go together— like oil and water, TV evangelists and integrity.

Church is a place, however, where interesting combinations do exist— young and old, rich and poor, in-crowd and outcast, black and white, Republican and Democrat. God's spirit working in us unites us in our purpose. We're not all alike, but we're all united in service and love.

See you at the drive-thru.

Star Wars '97
I don't ever carry much cash on me. The late Ted McCollum always teased me about not having any cash and having to charge a $5.00 lunch. So it was a big surprise one day this week when I had a $100.00 bill. When Tyler heard I had "a hundred bucks," he said: "Dad, you could buy two Millennium Falcons with that." For the uninitiated in *Star Wars* jargon, the Millennium Falcon is a spaceship in the *Star Wars*

Trilogy. And yes, they cost about $50.00 a piece at the local Wal-Mart.

It amazes me how much kids Tyler's age know about the *Star Wars* movies. In case you've forgotten, they came out some twenty or thirty years ago and have been re-released recently. Tyler and his friends know all the characters and lines in all the movies. In fact, they probably know more about Luke Skywalker, Darth Vader and Hans Solo than they do King David, the Apostle Paul and Simon Peter. They also know more lines from the movie than verses from the Bible. It's called marketing. The marketers of the *Star Wars* theme have done a remarkable job of reaching a new generation of fans. Of course, their success has cost me money. I've purchased several *Star Wars* figures for Tyler, and that, by the way, is the reason I never have any cash.

I've been thinking about marketing at the church. How much should we do? How do churches create interest without resorting to neon lights, blimps, bells and whistles? How do we get children as interested in the Bible characters as *Star Wars* figures? The greatest marketing tool we have at church is you. You and your testimony. If you show a lot of interest in the Bible characters, then maybe kids will too.

Church Cuisine
A primary school teacher asked her class to bring an example of a religious icon that their church uses. A Jewish boy smiled because he knew what he would bring; the Catholic girl smiled because she knew what she would bring, but the little Baptist boy looked

puzzled. "Show and Tell" arrived the next day. The teacher asked the first boy what he brought. He said, "I brought the Star of David." The teacher asked the little girl what she brought. She said, "I'm Catholic, and I brought a crucifix." Finally she asked the last little boy what he brought. He said, "I'm Baptist, and I brought a casserole."

Someone twisted the scripture passage to read, "Where two or three are gathered in my name there is food in the midst of them." People like to pick at us Baptists because we're always eatin'. We do more serving of food to others, however, than we do consuming. So many in our congregation have a wonderful ministry of "casseroles and Kleenex." Inevitably, when I go to see someone who has been through a crisis, they will say that "So and so just left. They brought supper." They also brought love, tenderness and compassion. Comes with the meal. They're not side orders, though. Main dish.

Towing Theology
Chattanooga, Tennessee, is renowned as a tourist attraction, having places like Lookout Mountain, Ruby Falls and Rock City (as in "See Rock City"). In recent years it has added things like the Discovery Museum and the Aquarium. On a recent trip to that lovely city, we discovered another reason to make the trek north: The International Towing and Recovery Museum. Believe it or not, there is such a place. The history of towing is on display, along with the Towing Hall of Fame, which prompted lots of questions for my ministerial mind. Isn't the church in the towing business? Yes. If the church had a tow truck, what

would it look like? Would it look like one of our deacons making a hospital visit? Or an ambassador making a house call to a prospect? Or a missions leader taking time with a child? Or would it look like you visiting with a neighbor, hearing about a recent heartbreak and offering your support and prayers? Yes, towing and recovery is our business!

Jesus told a parable about a man in a ditch (Luke 10). That man symbolizes people all over our community. Beaten. Bruised. Abused. Left for dead. Are you listening for their distress signal? Will you answer their 911 call? They are "broken down" along life's highway and might remain there forever unless you and I answer the call. The Good Samaritan "towed" the beaten man to safety (put him on a donkey) and helped him "recover" (gave to the innkeeper for his care). We can do no less.

Bar-ometer
I don't spend time hanging around bars. Whew! (I know you are relieved.) However, I recently read about the closing of a famous bar that got my attention. Harleys, a Manhattan institution that dates back to the 19th century, is closing. It became famous when they refused John D. Rockefeller's millions as he began snapping up leases for the construction of Rockefeller Center. The Harleys turned him down so the 70-story RCA building had to be built around the bar. Harleys was a place where the famous, such as Henry Kissinger, John Belushi, Howard Hughes and David Letterman have "hung out." However, in its closing, here's what people said about it: "It's the kind of bar where status

was left at the door. It's one of the few places where people didn't come to impress. They came to talk."

I guess bars are places where you can be yourself and talk about what troubles you. I am reminded of one of my favorite jokes. A horse walked into a bar and the bartender said: "Hey, hey, hey, why the long face?"

Aren't churches supposed to be places where status is left at the door? And where people don't come to impress? Paul says that in Christ there is "neither Jew nor Greek, slave nor free, male nor female" (Galatians 3:28). We're all one in Christ. Bars and churches have more in common than we might think.

Our Church
Children say the darndest things. Jacob Bryant, three-year-old son of Stacy and Rhonda Corley, has given me two gems lately. Last Wednesday he told me that he likes to go down our slide at church because from there "I can see God." A second quote came from Jacob at the city soccer fields. He walked up to Sheri and me and said, "You go to our church." BINGO. He got it right. Our church, not my church.

Our church. It doesn't belong to any one of us. Ultimately, it belongs to Christ. As Jacob grows older, he will understand more and more the complete implications of "our church." Romans 12 tells us to "weep with those who weep" and "rejoice with those who rejoice." An essential ingredient in being "our church" is that when our brothers and sisters suffer, we suffer with them. We feel their pain. Remember, "He bore 'our' infirmities" (Isaiah 53:4). Conversely, when they are happy, we are happy for them.

It's our church, not my church. When it becomes my church, then we expect it to serve us. An "our church" attitude means we serve it. Count on it. Jacob says so.

Taylor's Theology

I recently baptized one of our special children, Morgan Cantrell. Baptism is a symbol of a profound experience that shapes the remainder of our lives. The profundity of it is difficult to explain to children. However, four-year-old Taylor Smith seems to grasp it. As Pam talked to her son about that particular worship service, she asked him what he liked best. "When Morgan got wet," he said. Pam then began to explain to Taylor what it means to become a Christian, and why Christians are baptized. She felt as if she had done a very commendable job of explaining why Morgan "got wet." When daddy Marty got home that evening, Pam told him about the conversation with Taylor. He followed up and said, "Son, do you understand what happened to Morgan?" "Yes, Dad," he said, "she became a creature."

Taylor was correct. The apostle Paul would give a hearty amen to Taylor's theology. Paul says, "In Christ we are new creatures" (2 Corinthians 5:17). I say to children when talking about baptism that it means we are now clean on the inside. Could we learn from the children? Are we clean on the inside? Do we confess our sins so we can live like new creatures?

Steve Davis

I pray that each of our church's children will profess their faith in Christ and be baptized. I pray that we adults will follow their lead.

Volun-tears

A local elementary school had a Volunteer Day last Saturday. Sheri and Tyler were at the zoo, so I decided it would be a good time to do my volunteer work. Parents are encouraged to volunteer for a few hours each year. Upon entering the school lobby, I was greeted warmly and asked, "Do you want to work outside and plant pansies or go to the cafeteria and work on some games for teachers?" Easy call, I thought. I'd rather have a root canal than do yard work. So, off to the cafeteria I went.

I was given a sack complete with instructions on how to "cut and paste" this particular game for a third-grade class. Though I have several framed diplomas in my office, I could not make heads or tails of the instructions. Sally Tillman came to the rescue and not only "'splained" them to me but also let me borrow her scissors. No problem, I thought. Just a little cutting and pasting and I'm outta here. Two hours and forty-five minutes later I finished. That's right. Two hours and forty-five minutes. I had scissor cramps.

The experience not only added to my deepening appreciation for teachers, but also for volunteers. Just as the school needs volunteers, the church couldn't survive without them. Sunday School teachers. Mission and choir leaders. And a host of others. Every Sunday and Wednesday are volunteer days at church. Thanks.

10

Home Alone

When I was growing up, we got gasoline at a service station. A "service" station was a place where you drove your car up to the pump and from there someone "serviced" your car. That meant they put gas in it, checked under your hood and put air in your tires. That kind of service is long gone in our society. But a new type of service has emerged. I don't know when it began, but perhaps it was with pizza delivery.

Now, if you have a computer and a credit card, you can have all sorts of items delivered to your home: magazines, chips, movies, groceries, etc. Some of the companies delivering the goods are Food.com, Web Van, HomeGrocer.com and Kozmo.com, to name a few. I'm not sure if they deliver yet to Carrollton, but I don't think so. When they do, I guess we'll log on for some items, mostly milk and dog food. Those are the two things that we seem to always need. (Do you think they could deliver a sermon on Saturday night for an unprepared preacher?) I wonder how far this will go.

I know one thing they can't deliver: worship. The writer of Hebrews says: "Forsake not the assembling of yourselves together" (10:25). Our faith is not only God-centered, but also people-centered. Worship is vertical; that is, directed toward God. But there is the horizontal dimension. We worship with the people of God, hand in hand, raising our voices in song and prayer to God. And we hear his Word together and respond, not only individually, but communally. I know that a person can, theoretically, worship at home. But your greatest worship will be at church.

Whassup?
Hope you haven't missed the latest phrase to sweep the nation. It's more popular than "Just Do It" or "Is that your final answer?" The phrase was first used in beer commercials (wouldn't you know it?) and its pitchmen have become media darlings. The phrase is "Whassup" (the official, but not phonetic spelling). It's short for "What's up?" The phrase began 10 or 15 years ago among friends, but it is now sweeping the nation. These friends are now TV stars who have appeared on *The Today Show*, *The Tonight Show* and *Saturday Night Live*. And how does one properly pronounce "Whassup?" "You have to first of all be very enthusiastic," one of the founders explained. "It comes from the diaphragm. Relax the throat and release the tongue. And just belt it out. And the 'p' is silent."

Why not tell your neighbor "Whassup"? Let them know about a place—your church or mine—where one can experience love, acceptance and the Spirit of Christ? Children, youth, young and old alike are experiencing the resurrection life. Come be a part.

Seeing Red
Aren't there a few things we can always count on? The sky being blue. Green grass. Brown dirt. Pink flamingos. But now this: green ketchup. As most of you have heard by now, Heinz has announced the unthinkable. "Green is going to be a shocker for a lot of adults. But kids don't have those hang-ups," said a company spokesman.

After its share of the U.S. ketchup market dropped to 43% in the last few years, Heinz embarked on this new green ketchup campaign. Heinz did some research on focus groups and found out that kids would like to see ketchup in some color besides red. They considered blue but settled on green because of its "kitchen logic." A food analyst (I don't know what a food analyst is, but it sure sounds like a great job) said, "It will certainly sell on St. Patrick's Day. They're trying to keep the product contemporary to a new generation."

Doesn't that speak volumes (or ounces) to the modern church? We struggle with, on the one hand, clinging to time-honored traditions and, on the other hand, trying to reach and stay contemporary with the 21st century. I don't care to go back to the 1st century where slavery abounded and women were treated like second-class citizens. Neither do I want to return to a century ago when members were expelled from our church for dancing. But I like traditions. They are anchors. Cornerstones. We need some. So do we give people what they want (green ketchup) or what they need (tomato soup)? Just wondering.

Who Wants to Be a …?
It doesn't take much to excite a preacher. How about a Sunday afternoon ice storm? Or a heated baptistry? Or a matching tie and hanky? Well, what about a call from a lawyer who says, "Pastor, we've settled Mr. Bailey's will, and he has left it all to the church." "All? How much is all?" asks the Reverend. "Sixty," says the lawyer. "Sixty thousand?" the Reverend inquires. "No, sixty million," says the lawyer. Pause. Long pause. Dial 911. Cardiac arrest. Clergy crisis.

I can't vouch for the above conversation, but the facts are these. Warren Bailey died and left $60 million to the St. Mary's United Methodist Church in St. Mary's, Georgia. The church has an annual budget of $285,000! Because Mr. Bailey left no instructions on how the money should be spent, I have some suggestions for them:

1. Pastor putting green on back lawn of parsonage;
2. Swiss Alps sabbatical for all staff members;
3. Steak and lobster every Wednesday night at church, and
4. Jacuzzi in pastor's study.

Seriously, the pastor at St. Mary's, Rev. McAleer, is concerned with how all that money will affect his congregation. He worries that greed might overcome the parishioners. He asked the very poignant question, "How do we remain a Christian Church?"

It's really a good question for all of us wealthy, American Christians. Have Christian people or churches ever known such wealth and prosperity as we have today? I doubt it. How do we remain authentically Christian and not get consumed with our possessions? The Bible encourages the tithe as a way of ensuring that we have our priorities straight. Try it.

Blind Dates
I got married when I was 35, so I know a little bit about dating, in particular, "blind dates." Be careful when someone wants to "set you up" with someone who is "cute." Everyone is "cute" to someone. I trembled when someone said "she's cute, she makes her own

clothes, and all the girls like her." When you hear that, guys, run for your lives.

I read recently about a new concept called Turbo Dating, a form of blind dating. An equal number of Jewish men and women sit in pairs at stations along a table and kibitz at the Marcus Jewish Community Center in Atlanta. Every seven minutes a bell rings and they rotate to new partners. At the end of the evening they give each person a thumbs up or down and indicate whether they want to see one again. If both agree, they get phone numbers by email a few days later. The cost is $18 for JCC members and $25 for nonmembers.

First impressions are very important and no less so in church work. People form first impressions in those crucial moments after arriving at the church. Greeters, ushers and loving, smiling members convey a message. For some people, visiting a new church can be as scary as going on a blind date. I'm glad to report that most people who visit our wonderful church give it a thumbs up. Thanks.

What's in a Name?
I get tired of people talking about the "good ole days," but let's talk about the good ole days. Days gone by when stadiums and arenas were named after famous people (JFK, Joe Louis, Connie Mack) or had some cool moniker (Three Rivers, The Stick, The Forum). All that has changed. It must be a sign of the Apocalypse. Stadiums and arenas are now christened with the names of corporate America. Sunday afternoon I watched a portion of the Raiders/Ravens NFL playoff game. "Live from Network Associates Coliseum," said the

announcer. Huh? The Baltimore Ravens play in a stadium called PSI Net. Are you kidding me? Other examples that the end is near: the Arizona Diamondbacks play at Bank One Ballpark and the Seattle Mariners at Safeco Field. And get this: Louisville plays college football at Papa John's Cardinal Stadium.

I don't like this trend. Sure hope it never comes to the church. AllTell Baptist Church. (Sounds like a church where gossip abounds.) Quolcomm Community Church. RCA Presbyterian. E*Trade Episcopalian. Baptist churches are usually named after their street location (Roopville Road), neighborhood (Shady Grove) or after some biblical/theological term (Grace, Trinity or Beulah). Usually churches named Unity have split off from another congregation. What does your church's name mean to you and to those who drive by your congregation?

WWW.WORSHIP
My idea of a good time is a trip to The Varsity, Atlanta's most famous restaurant, followed by a Braves game. Actually, just a trip to The Varsity would qualify. It's a long drive into Atlanta for a chilidog, but then it's not just any dog. The Varsity has a special ambiance, alone with some great, greasy food. Tyler likes to order a "naked dog," i.e. plain hot dog, or perhaps he just enjoys hearing the fast-talking waiters yelling "naaaked dawg." You also have your choice of "heavy weight" (hot dog with extra chili), "bag of rags" (potato chips) or "strings" (French fries). We love the atmosphere and food at The Varsity.

The Varsity now has its own interactive web site which chronicles the history of this fast-food landmark, plus a menu complete with hats, T-shirts and gift certificates. It has audio that simulates the sounds at the real place.

Don't know about you, but I'd much rather go to the real Varsity than visit www.thevarsity.com. I want the sights, sounds, smells (and indigestion) that go along with the place. I want to be at church for the same reasons (minus the indigestion). I don't worship well at home, at the computer, on the lake or at the golf course. I want the real deal. Our sanctuary is a special place— complete with sights and sounds that inspire worship. It's important that we be in worship on Sunday. Without it our spiritual lives will be relegated to the B-Team. We will never make "the varsity."

Mowing Mania
Looking for a new hobby that combines the thrill of racing with the satisfaction of lawn mowing? Have I got an answer for you: The National Lawn Mower Racing Series. No kidding! These people race riding lawn mowers (according to a recent *Sports Illustrated* article).[1] They meet on soccer fields and baseball diamonds all across America. They don racing gear and helmets, and when the gun goes off, they crank up their mowers and take off, reaching speeds of 8 mph. You could join the fun. All you need is the $5 entry fee, a bladeless riding mower and proof that you haven't tinkered with the engine. One of the grassroots leaders of the sport is a guy named Dubba G (a.k.a. Garret Gray) from Duncanville, Texas, who said: "It's all a

---

[1] Rick Riley, *Sports Illustrated,* October 2000.

redneck could want. You drive 1,200 miles so you can drive your lawn mower in circles, get bugs in your teeth and have cold, adult beverages." Dubba G said he discovered this spectacle on the Nashville Network one night and screamed to his wife: "Honey, get in here! I've found my people!"

I've found my people! What a statement for us at church to hear. Now, I'm not comparing church to lawn mower racing, and I acknowledge the differences between the congregations of both, but ... I wonder if people walk in to our church and say the same. Many do. Everybody just wants a place to belong - a place where one can be honest and open, without pretense. One such place is the church. The Greek term <u>Koinonia</u> means "fellowship." It describes the church, and in a loose sense, Dubba G's "people" in the racing series.

"Worshippers, start your engines."

"Hurted So Bad"
Kids can say things in ways that we adults only wish we could. The words of seven-year- old Joshua Tucker are echoing off the walls of my study as I pen this article. Words that were read in a courtroom are words that should be heard in the church. Joshua's mom was killed by a hit-and-run driver, and the judge dismissed the charges against the man. Joshua wrote a letter to the judge that was delivered by his grandmother. His letter to the judge included these words: " ... When I hear people talking about it, it makes me real sad. Even when we had the funeral, I felt very sad and I wanted to just scream in the church. It hurted me so bad. I just wanted to scream in church."

Have you ever hurt so bad that you wanted to scream in church? I'll bet you have. We don't know the depth of pain that others seated on the pew next to us carry. The old spiritual says it best, "Nobody knows the trouble I've seen." So true. Nobody knows the long nights staring at the clock. Nobody knows how hard you have tried to overcome your own personal demons. Nobody knows the fears that paralyze you or the shame that binds you. Nobody knows. You wish they did. You wish you could cry out in church, "cause it hurted me so bad." Church should be a place where we can cry, and our cries will not go unattended. The words of a Ken Medema song come to mind: "If this is not a place where tears are understood, where shall I go; where can I go to cry?"

That old spiritual ends with these words: "Nobody knows but Jesus." Amen.

Transportation Theology
"I come from Alabama with a banjo on my knee" are the lyrics to a once-popular tune. It's true for me, minus the banjo. Born and raised in that wonderful state. Proud of it, too. Though we were 49th in about everything (thank the Lord for Mississippi), we were first in the things that mattered, like football. I've heard lots of "Alabama" jokes because I have lived in other states for many years. Funny how we never told them on ourselves; perhaps because we couldn't remember or didn't understand the punch line. I find them not so humorous. For example, you know you're from Alabama if:

    1. "Vacation" means going to a family reunion.
    2. You know several people who have hit a deer.

3. Stores don't have shopping carts; they have buggies.
4. You use "fix" as a verb, but you aren't repairing anything.
5. The minister calls on "Bubba" to lead in prayer and five men stand up to pray.

And now this. If you're from Alabama, you probably ride alone. Alabama leads the nation in the percentages of people who drive to work by themselves. (OK, no jokes about why.) A spokesman for AAA said: "They like the independence the automobile provides. They are able to smoke. They are able to eat in the car. They are able to listen to their own kind of music."

Two comments. One, I appreciate the value of solitude. Jesus spent much time alone with God in prayer and meditation, and if we don't, then our spiritual lives will suffer. Two, we are made for community. We weren't made for "eatin'," "drinkin'" and "listenin' to music" alone. The church is a car-poolin' kind of place. We fellowship together. Pray and worship together. Minister together. You might call it "care-pooling." Need a ride?

"Reel" Worship
Been to the movies lately? I'm intrigued by all the hype in the promos or blurbs for the upcoming flicks. For example, for the movie *The Sum of All Fears*, the blurb was "Grabs you by the throat and never lets go." Huh? Is that supposed to make me want to go? "The perfect summer movie" is how the film *Bad Company* was promoted. What constitutes a perfect summer movie, as opposed to, say an autumn one? And what about the hit,

Divine Secrets of the Ya-Ya Sisterhood? "Simply divine" is the blurb for this summer blockbuster. Divine? That is a lot for a movie to live up to. The hype has become too much. Stop the presses. What's next? "Three thumbs up."

We in the church struggle with the issue of worship versus entertainment. Are we going to start hyping worship, as in, "One hour of exhilarating, non-stop fun?" "Come to FBC where the pastor puts on an Oscar-winning performance." "A worship rush from Prelude to Postlude."

Worship is not about you or me. A pep rally it is not. It is not about making us feel good or giving us a rush. Worship *is* about entering into God's presence and praising, listening to, and honoring God. See you Sunday for a meaningful worship experience. And that's no hype.

Suit Sermon
Sheri was startled. It was 2:30 a.m. when she sat up in bed, "What was that?" The noise that had awakened her was a loud thud. I, on the other hand, can sleep through a hurricane. Sheri thought someone had broken into our home. Needless to say, we were relieved to discover that instead, some brackets in my closet had given way and the thud was the sound of suits crashing to the floor. Suits? Yes, lots of them. Ministers have sermons and suits. I have as many suits as Elizabeth Taylor has had husbands. I have funeral suits (dark ones). Wedding suits. Winter ones. Summer ones. When they fell, it sounded like all my chili cooking awards hitting the floor at once. Hah. Would you believe Bill Gates'

wallet hitting the floor? The brackets were cheap plastic ones, and I simply loaded too many suits for them to bear up.

When you and I get overloaded, we too will come crashing down without proper support. Cheap plastic brackets will not stand the weight of the burdens we bear. What kind of support do you have? Prayer? Faith? Church friends? I've heard it said many a time, "I don't know how I would have made it without my church friends." Amen.

Specialization

Everything in our society is so highly specialized. Have you tried to buy orange juice lately? Pulp? No pulp? Low acid orange juice? (How is that possible?) Doctors specialize: orthopedist, podiatrist, cardiologist, etc. Engineers do too—civil, electrical, mechanical, etc. If you doubt me on this, take note of the **Babies 'R Us** stores. Entire stores specializing in nothing but baby stuff—strollers, car seats, bottles, cribs, changing tables and millions of diapers. Aisle after aisle. If they don't have it, forget it. You can't find it.

What's next? A store made just for me, **Geezers 'R Us**. Complete with the latest walkers, canes, hearing aids, robes, dentures, slippers, remote controls, Ben Gay, and all the Geritol I need.

Churches, too, tend to specialize in certain things. What does your church do especially well? Worship? Outreach? We had better be good at reaching the babies and the geezers and all the generations in between. The church should be a place where the youngest to the oldest know, respect and trust one another.

Blessed 'R Us

"All Shook Up"

Recently I bought a new CD: Elvis' number one hits. I like Elvis. Oh, I know he's been dead for some time now, though I would swear I saw him at a Po Folks restaurant a few years ago. Looked just like him. Anyway, when I played the CD for Tyler and it came to "Don't Be Cruel," he asked incredulously, "Do you actually like that?" Sure, it's the music I grew up with. Besides, I love music with great meaning and depth, songs that explore the philosophical and spiritual meaning of life, as opposed to this "shallow" modern music. "Don't Be Cruel." Now there's a song with character and depth.

> *Don't be cruel, ooh ooh, to a heart that's true. I don't want no other love—baby it's just you I'm thinking of.*

Or how about that deep, philosophical tune by Elvis, "All Shook Up"?

> *Well bless my soul, what's wrong with me? I'm itching like a man on a fuzzy tree. My friends say I'm acting wild as a bug— I'm in love, I'm all shook up.*

OK. So, maybe, Elvis' music doesn't exactly probe the inner recesses of the human heart or address significant societal issues. I still like "Hound Dog." Perhaps there is some deep hidden symbolism in the words.

> *You ain't nothing but a hound dog, crying all the time. You ain't never caught a rabbit, you ain't no friend of mine.*

Seriously, the music I like even more than Elvis is church music, in particular, church hymns. Each stanza contains rich, theological insights. My favorite hymn, as some of you know, is "When I Survey the Wondrous Cross." The first verse is:

> *When I survey the wondrous cross, On which the Prince of Glory died, My richest gain I count but loss, And pour contempt on all my pride.*

Ponder those words and the remaining verses as well, and you'll be "All Shook Up."

Dreamland

On a recent visit from our friends, Robert and Rhonda Cotton, who now live in Tuscaloosa, Alabama, Robert brought us a jar of Dreamland BBQ sauce. Now if you haven't heard of Dreamland, then you aren't a connoisseur of BBQ ribs. Dreamland certainly is the most famous restaurant in the "sovereign state of Alabama" (as a well-known former governor used to say). Dreamland is in an old house, off the beaten path, that has served BBQ ribs forever. In recent years it has become popular with the general public and is the restaurant of choice for the sports crowd. Several years back I took Sheri and Tyler there for the "cultural experience." It was all of that and more. All they serve at Dreamland is ribs, bread and drinks. That's all. The menu is simply there to help you determine how much you want. Well, Sheri gazed at the menu so long (too long) that the 300-pound waiter finally said in exasperation, "Ma'am, all we have is ribs, ribs, and ribs. When you decide what you want, you let me know." We laughed till we cried. Well, Sheri finally ordered, and we got our ribs. Believe me, those ribs were goooooooooood. I'm going to grill out this summer and use the Dreamland sauce that Robert gave me, but I'm guessing they won't taste as good as Dreamland's. That will have something to do with the ability of the chef and also the place in which they are served. We could never create at my home the ambiance, the feeling, the culture of that old house turned restaurant.

I love Easter music. I love it anytime and anyplace, but I especially love it when I sing it with you in our sanctuary. There is something special about certain songs, sung with certain people, sung in certain places. There is a certain ambiance, feeling and culture about our church. Like the usher at church said, "All we serve is worship, worship, and worship here at Dreamland Baptist Church."

Little Rascals
I recently watched the movie *Little Rascals* with some children at our church. It took me back, of course, to the wonderful TV series by the same name that I enjoyed as a kid. In the movie, the guys, Spanky, Alfalfa, and the gang, have a club called the **He-Man Womun Haters Club**. They took solemn vows never to speak to or associate with a girl. Kissing one would have amounted to heresy. Well, there are really two plots going on simultaneously in the movie. One, Alfalfa has a crush on Darla, but, of course, doesn't want the guys to know. Two, the gang's clubhouse burns down, and they spend the remainder of the movie plotting and scheming to get the money to rebuild it. Regarding Alfalfa and Darla, the guys find our about their romance, threaten to disown Alfalfa and accuse him of the worst kinds of heresy. In the end, however, the guys change their minds about girls because Darla saves the day for them

in a race, one that nets them $500 for the rebuilding of their clubhouse. So, girls are finally admitted to the club. I couldn't help but note the parallel to the role of women in the church. Though they have been in the "club," they have not been allowed in many churches to express their spiritual gifts or to serve in any leadership positions. Thanks to the Darlas of the church world, that is changing. Regarding the loss of the clubhouse and subsequent plans to rebuild it, another wonderful parallel to the church emerged. Guess what they discovered? They still had a club even without a clubhouse. Their friendships transcended the loss of their building. A church is still a church even without the sanctuary.

Nuisance News
With a headline like that, I could be talking about a lot of folk, so don't take it personally. I really didn't have you in mind though, 'cause the inspiration for this article came from a recent report in the AJC regarding "nuisance tickets" being issued by NYC policemen. It seems a crime wave is sweeping the Big Apple, and its citizens aren't too happy about it. Police have recently ticketed people for such nuisance crimes as sitting on a milk crate on the sidewalk. Jesse Taveras is the 19-year-old who faces a court date and a fine of $161 for the milk crate caper. Somebody was fined $50 for taking up two seats on a train. Another citizen had to cough up 50 bucks for feeding pigeons in the park. Crystal Rivera got a $50 ticket for sitting on the steps at a train station. Well, you get the picture. Critics say these tickets are just the city's way of closing New York's $3.8 billion budget gap.

All of this got me to thinking about church. What if the church started issuing nuisance fines for certain misdeeds? Have you ever sat beside someone in worship who sang like Roseanne Barr? $50 fine. How about dozing like Rip Van Winkle during the sermon? That will cost you, big time. One hundred dollars in the plate should do. Or what about a member parking in the Guest Parking spots? You'll be out $100 for the Lord's work. Well, this has the makings of great stewardship campaign in the fall: "Be a Nuisance for Christ."

Seriously, all of us have the potential to be a nuisance or to "rub others the wrong way." Paul's statement in 1 Corinthians 13 is "love is patient." It is, especially with those who would annoy us.

Ya'll Come
I like Bishop Fred Caldwell's spunk and tenacity. I'm not sure about his methods. The bishop is a black minister in Shreveport, Louisiana, who grew tired of seeing so few whites in his predominantly black church that he has offered to pay whites $5 an hour out of his own pocket for attending Sunday services and $10 an hour for Thursday night services. He has apparently gotten mostly positive response from his parishioners and from whites who have told him they will attend his services for free. Perhaps people are responding favorably because they sense sincerity in his appeal.

All of this has gotten me to thinking about what we could offer to entice people to come to church. Free parking? No church library late fees? A personalized set of offering envelopes? Short, interesting sermons? (Well, three out of four ain't bad.) Any appeal we make for someone to attend any church should be grounded in a spiritual concern for his or her well being, which we sincerely believe can be met in the warmth of the church. So, come and see for yourself. Five bucks says you will like it.

Safety First

We as a society have gone nuts over safety. We have home security systems and floodlights, plus a ferocious dog to guard our place. Seat belts aren't enough for our cars; we now have airbags and automatic locks. We "baby proof" our homes to keep the precious children safe. Well, you get the point. I have some information on safety that might interest you. To really be safe, you should avoid riding in automobiles because they account for 20% of all fatal accidents. On the other hand, to ensure safety, you can't stay at home because 17% of all accidents occur at home. However, if you choose to walk on the sidewalk or streets, be aware that 14% of all accidents happen to pedestrians. So, that is not a safe choice either. Neither is traveling by air, rail, or water because 16% of all accidents involve these forms of transportation. That leaves 33% and guess what? Thirty-two percent of all deaths occur in hospitals. At all costs, avoid hospitals. There is some good news in all this paranoia. Are you ready for this? Only .001% of all deaths occur in worship services in church, and these are usually related to some previous physical disorder. It is a fact that a lot of folk thought that bad preaching would "do them in," but so far no direct link between a bad homily and the death of the saints has been ascertained. So logic would tell us that worship is a very safe place to be.

Given the statistics cited above, when I tell you that our sanctuary is "drop-dead" gorgeous, you won't take me literally, will you?

See you Sunday in the church of your choice. It could save your life!

Prison Plan
You'll be glad to know that I've never been in jail. At least not yet. However, I came mighty close recently when I went into a fast-food restaurant with Natalie (our two-year-old). The young girl behind the counter asked me, "Is that your daughter or granddaughter?" You would have been proud of me. I could have lost it. I could have gotten a "Go to Jail" card. "Do not pass Go. Go directly to jail." Do I look old enough to have a granddaughter? Don't answer that. Seriously, her comment didn't bother me. Really. Well, I did give her a mean look. But I did nothing that would land me in the slammer.

What would a church do if their minister did wind up in jail? The apostle Paul spent a lot of time in prison because of his Christian faith, and the churches he had founded seemed to do well without him. The church at Philippi is a good example. Though in jail at the time of the writing of the epistle bearing the Philippian name, Paul was confident in the church. Or should I say, confident in God. "And my God will supply every need of yours according to his riches in glory in Christ Jesus" (4:19). If our faith is in the living Christ and not the minister, then a church can survive even the most difficult of times. Every church needs a "prison plan," and that plan is to depend completely upon God's provision. I have no plans to break the law and wind up behind bars unless one more person asks me "Is that your…?"

Birds of a Feather

They're back. Some of you may not know they were ever here. Others didn't notice when they left. Some have observed their return. Well, believe me they are back in full force. I'm talking about the pigeons on the church steeple. If you don't believe me, then go to the front of the church and look up. (On second thought that may not be such a good idea.) For the last several years they have been hanging out at the Methodist church, much to our delight. I thought they made great Methodists. But now they are Baptist birds once again. How to get rid of them is now our problem. I suggest that we capture them, baptize them and make them church members. Then we would only see them twice a year, at Christmas and Easter. (Ha!) Or perhaps we could play "I'll Fly Away" on the carillon.

Then again, maybe we shouldn't worry so about them at all, because churches have always attracted an odd assortment of birds beneath the steeple, in addition to on it. Every church has its share of buzzards and turkeys that congregate beneath the steeple. As determined as we are to scare the birds off the steeple, we should be equally determined to attract the wayward and odd birds who gather beneath it in need of help. Pigeons are attracted to our steeple for reasons I don't understand, but people, hurting people, are attracted to our steeple for reasons I do understand. They believe that beneath the steeple they will find love, acceptance and understanding. They come to the steeple to find faith, family and fellowship. They believe that beneath the steeple is a sanctuary, a place of refuge. Let's make sure the nest is warm and large enough for all the odd birds who come our way. In the meantime, pray that our parish pigeons will soon become Presbyterians or Episcopalians.

Gospel Bird
Need a job? It would be a great place to live and work. It seems the good folk in Key West, Florida, are looking to hire a chicken catcher. Said Assistant City Manager John James, "He's got to be fast, he's got to be brave and he's got to be smarter than the chickens." Oh well, maybe I'd better stick to preaching. Chicken overpopulation has been an ongoing issue for Key West, so much so that a few years ago the city called a "chicken summit" and decided to round up about 200 of the fowl creatures and ship them to a bird sanctuary. But that was only a drop in the proverbial (KFC) bucket. The official estimate of Key West's chicken flock is 2,000, and they are everywhere, as in hotel parking lots and restaurant terraces. (If these birds are so smart, why are they hanging out at restaurants where chicken is served fried, baked and with Parmesan?)

I have decided that we will never have a chicken problem here in Georgia. Too many Baptists. If a chicken hangs out anywhere near a Baptist church, it is a goner. I've eaten more fried chicken and deviled eggs at our church than there are rocks on Mars. I guess that is why we have dubbed our fowl friends the "gospel bird."

Seriously, nothing symbolizes our fellowship and abiding relationships more than the meals we share

31

together. In recent weeks we have buried eight of our outstanding members and after or before each funeral, our Bereavement Team has prepared a meal for the grieving family. Invariably, the family thanks the church for that wonderful ministry. And invariably we eat fried chicken and lots of other wonderful foods. It is part of a ministry that we have called "Kleenex and casseroles." These women who do the cooking have many talents that they share with the church, and one of them is cooking chicken. Many thanks from the leader of the "flock."

Graceland
In the past, I often wondered what Elvis would look like if he were alive today. Now I know, thanks to Lee Laster's stirring impersonation at a recent Valentine's Banquet. Yes, I said Lee Laster, recent deacon chairman. In case you missed the banquet and are wondering, Elvis has slowed down a bit. Instead of shaking his pelvis, he shakes his walker. The AARP ladies go wild.

I was a huge Elvis fan years ago and still enjoy his music, but I no longer make annual pilgrimages to his home, Graceland. I have sold my pink Cadillac and given away my blue suede shoes. But I have been known to say, "thank you, thank you very much" after a good golf shot. Seriously, people take this Elvis stuff to the extreme. Urban legends abound. One story is that a blue light appeared over the Presley home in Tupelo, Mississippi, the night Elvis was born. (Was he born in a K-Mart?) A popular Elvis legend is that a truck driver picked up a hitchhiker going to Memphis and was startled to see Elvis sitting beside him. All of these legends are designed to keep his memory alive.

Keeping memories alive is what I hope we can continue to do at church. We don't need made-up stories or imagined sightings to remember some of the great people who have passed away recently—people who really were legends to our church home, our "Grace" land. I've never had to embellish a eulogy or make someone larger in death than they were in life. My church is grieving over the loss of many fine members in recent years, but their memory inspires us to live lives like unto theirs. Thanks Lee for dressing and singing like (sort of) the King and reminding us to keep the memories alive.

The Atticus Example
We recently saw the play "To Kill a Mockingbird," which is being performed at our Cultural Arts center. Good play. As you might remember, a small town Alabama lawyer in the 30's is representing a black man who has been falsely accused of the rape of a white woman. The lawyer's name is Atticus Finch, and as you can imagine, his decision to represent this client has caused much local criticism. His daughter, Scout, is of course, very proud of her dad and very protective of him. One of the great things about her dad she said was that he was always the same in the courtroom, at home or on the street. In other words, he wasn't one person in court and then a totally different person when away from work. What a testimony. I have known so many pastors over the years who are totally different persons when they preach. I know one who said that when he preaches, he gets behind the pulpit and "pitches a fit."

Maybe he pitches fits at home, I don't know. I have tried to be like Atticus Finch and be the same person at church and at home. It's tough to do. The ministry almost invites hypocrisy because it is so easy to fake it. It's not easy to fake being a plumber because it shows up in your work. Same for being a surgeon. But ministers can quickly learn to fake it by making God a three-syllable word and spicing conversations with a few "praise the Lords" and throwing in an occasional biggie like "eschatology," and suddenly we sound ministerial. However, serving a church where people are generally very transparent is refreshing. In a sense, we hold each other accountable. As we each strive to be the same person at home, work and at church, that consistency rubs off. I honestly believe that the more honest, open and transparent we are, the closer we will be to God.

"Backslidin' Blues"
I love music, though I wasn't particularly blessed with talent in that area. Most types of music I appreciate. I love church music, especially hymns and anthems by our great choir. I'm fond of the music that I grew up with, namely, 60's classics. Country music was never my favorite, but in recent years I have come to appreciate its style and lyrics. Whenever I need sermon material, a country music song is only a radio away. I recently became aware of the lyrics of Del McCoury's "Backslidin' Blues." One of the lines goes like this: "I've quit goin' to church and gone back to sinning since you put me out with the trash." I wondered if those lyrics reflect a feeling that many have in our culture, that church is not a place you go when you feel hurt or worthless. I contrast that thinking with the lyrics of the beautiful song by Ken Medema, "If This Is Not a Place."

One of its lines is, "If this is not a place where my tears are understood, where can I go to cry?" Is Del McCoury's way of thinking the way it really is or how he perceives it to be?

It seems to me that if a church is not compassionate towards the hurting then we might as well close the doors. If there is anything that characterized the life of Jesus, it was a welcoming heart for the hurting. And the hurting always felt that in Jesus, they would find an attentive ear and a receptive heart. If the church is going to look at all like Jesus, then "sinners" had better be welcome inside its doors. So let's make a special effort to welcome all the "backsliders" into the house of the Lord!

All Tied Up
I had a professor in seminary who wore a coat and tie to class everyday. Those who knew him well said he mowed the yard in formal attire. Others questioned whether he slept in them. On a recent Sunday I preached at a sister church in town in a pulpit swap. It just so happened that they have been promoting casual dress for the summer. So I preached in only a sport coat with no tie. It was a bit awkward for me. I felt like a football player without a helmet. Or Dennis Rodman without tattoos.

I read about a recent study of doctors who wear neckties to achieve a look of professionalism. The study noted that physicians' neckties often brush across patients and bedding and thus carry pathogens. One in four carried Staphylococcus aureus (Is that some sort of sin?). The study questioned whether wearing a necktie was in the best interest of the patient. So, if the minister always wears a necktie, is it in the best interest of the parishioner? All germs aside, I seldom wear a necktie during the week because I want to look like a normal guy and relate well to everyone.

Many people at our church dress casually every Sunday. You see less and less formal clothing at church. I don't mind casual. But I don't like sloppy. Sloppy says you don't care. Sloppy says that it is not important enough to look good. I say that going into the house of the Lord is very important, and we should dress like it. I'm not hung up on coat and ties and starched shirts. I am hung up on trying to look clean and neat for something as significant as the worship of God. However, the Bible reminds us that God doesn't look on the outward appearance, but rather looks on the heart (1 Samuel 16:7). God is more concerned that our hearts aren't starched.

CHRISTIAN LIVING

Steve Davis

Christian Living

Character Flaw

On a recent trip home to Alabama, I browsed through some old scrapbooks and came upon my elementary school report cards. Thought I might show them to Tyler. He's in the second grade, so I checked out my second grade report card. Teacher: Mrs. Prophet. I scanned over to the behavior section. Under the heading "Excessive Talking" was a check mark for the first six weeks. Same for the second six weeks. And the third. Must be a mistake. So I checked my first and third grade report cards. Same thing. I decided not to show Tyler my report cards! I've been accused of lots of things in my life ... but never "excessive talking." Verbose? Loquacious? Blabber mouth? Not me. I found the report card shocking. Sheri found it amusing.

The teacher's name was Mrs. Prophet, right? Perhaps she was making a prophetic statement. (How did she know I would become a preacher?) Perhaps she gave everybody in the class a checkmark under "Excessive Talking." Or maybe my best friend Bob (a.k.a. "Sly") was talking to me, and I got caught responding. Surely there must be some rational explanation for this character flaw that I possessed in the late '50s. WRONG.

Wouldn't we all be better off admitting our character flaws, whether in '99 or '59? I've got some, how about you? The Bible calls character flaws sin and says we all have them (Romans 3:23). My son knows I have some because he lives with me everyday. Those who are closest to us know us best. On second thought, I'm going to show Tyler the report card and say, "Son, did I ever tell you that in second grade I walked just five miles to school in the snow."

Extra Mile

I have never been to Lancaster, Pennsylvania. In fact, I have never been to Pennsylvania, that I can recall. But I have fondness for Lancaster because of some high school kids that I have never met. It seems that when some kids at Lampeter-Strasburg High School heard about the damage that Hurricane Katrina caused to Long Beach High School and Pass Christian High School in Mississippi, they decided to take action.

What started with a phone call of "What can we do to help?" has turned into something that made this preacher tear up. The answer to the question was not what they expected. The answer was that they had lots of donated supplies. "No more pencils, please. What we really need is a party for these kids." You see, the kids were so down after losing everything and needed a school party to revive their spirits.

So, the idea of a homecoming dance was hatched. The students at Lampeter-Strasburg began the drive for cash and other needed items, such as 400 party dresses. Food was donated and T-shirts with the two school logos were made. A local bus company gave reduced rates, and some 40 students boarded a bus in Pennsylvania for the long ride to the Gulf Coast. Said one 18 year-old senior from Long Beach, "It is going to put some of my life back together." Said another Mississippi student, "...them actually coming down here is just really unbelievable. We are really grateful."

I've heard about Christians going the extra mile, but how about 1,168 miles?

Tight Fit
I wore some jeans Sunday afternoon to a college baseball game. Seems I have only one pair and hadn't worn them in a while. Sheri says, "Honey, we need to get you some new blue jeans." Translation: Those don't fit! Either (a) I have grown or (b) they have shrunk. "A" is the correct answer. Maybe I will get some new Levi's.

It seems the Levi Strauss Company is now offering computer-fit, custom-sized jeans. For a certain fee, you can have you own "made to fit" jeans delivered in just three weeks. What a deal!

Guess what? God has been in the customization business for a long, long time. There is no "one size fits all" philosophy in the Christian faith. We are each "uniquely made" in the image of God (Genesis 1:27-28).

But "uniquely made" doesn't mean that the "fabric" is perfect. In fact, we all have fabric that is "frayed." God accepts us with all our irregularities and gives us his blessing.

"All God's chillun' got customized Levi's."

Liturgical Movement
These times they are a-changing. Remember the dance craze that swept the nation a few years ago called the "Macarena"? (If you didn't see it, your TV must have

been on the blink.) My five-year-old son had a tape of the song and all the accompanying dance moves. He tried to teach mom and dad a few of the moves. Good luck. We ministerial types don't know much about dancing. We don't even use the word in church. We call it "liturgical movement."

I sometimes feel like I'm out of touch with all the changes in our society. The last dance I learned was the "Twist." Or was it the "Charleston"? I missed the disco era. I was in seminary at the time, and we seminarians didn't dare frequent the disco halls. We were afraid we might run into some sin.

What do we Christians do with this whole cultural issue? How much of it do we embrace? Reject? Defend? Change? Not all of our culture is bad. Much is good. We are called to be "in the world but not of the world." The scripture teaches: "Do not love the world or the things in the world" (1 John 2:15).

Food Fight
I used to drive Tyler and three other neighborhood kids to school. One day, I noticed the kids were unusually quiet. I'm not real good at entertaining kids. I tried to get them to sing along with me to tunes on the oldies station. But they wouldn't have any of that. So they sat there. They were probably wishing that Sheri were driving because she played word games with them. They liked that. I was boring to them, I suppose.

Well, halfway to school that day, Tyler pulled a Tootsie Roll out of his lunch sack. (The Tootsie Roll was fully wrapped.) Impulsively, I grabbed it and threw it to the back seat and yelled, "Food fight!" They threw it back to the front. Back. Front. Back. Front. For the remainder of the ride, I heard laughter, giggles and joy from all the kids as we played "Tootsie Roll Keep-Away." If they think that was fun, wait till tomorrow: spaghetti.

To relate to kids you've got to, in a sense, become one. I guess it applies to any age group, whether children or seniors. You have to find common ground on which to talk and relate if you are going to have an impact on them. Perhaps that is what Paul meant when he said, "I have become all things to all men, that I may by all means save some" (I Corinthians 9:22). I take that to mean that if we want to have an influence upon the world, we'd better make an effort to relate to all people. After all, God became one of us in the Incarnation in order to make us new people.

Hostages
When we go on trips or vacations, I do most of the driving. This form held true several years ago on our trip to Texas. Occasionally Sheri will drive to give me some relief, and when she does, I may go to the backseat with Tyler. Of course, once you let your spouse have the wheel, then you have given up some measure of control over your vacation.

Tyler and I found ourselves being held hostage in the backseat somewhere in East Texas. Not long after Sheri began driving, we passed a sign that said "Pottery Outlet." Uh oh. We were helpless. The car just automatically took the exit for the pottery store. There was wailing and gnashing of teeth from the guys. But to no avail. In spite of our protests, Tyler and I found ourselves looking at pots and silk flowers on our vacation. What kind of vacation is it when you stop at more pottery outlets than golf courses?

We decided to make the most of a bad situation; you know, make lemonade out of lemons. So we watched a man actually make one of the pots. It's a fascinating process. As I watched him work, I couldn't help but think about the passage in Jeremiah about God as the potter. Guess who is to be the clay, moist and pliable? The image of God taking us in his hands and molding us into his vessels is a great one.

So, I take back all the horrible things I have said about pottery outlets. But I do wonder if there aren't some theological insights to be gained at beaches and golf courses.

Elvis Imitators
Elvis is dead. The media gives us constant reminder of his passing. Can you believe it has been thirty-plus years since his death? Can you remember where you were when you heard the news? I can. If you were as big a fan as I was, you will never forget.

I'm still a fan, sort of. I remember the 45 rpm record of "Hound Dog" that I had as a child. And yes, I skipped Sunday night church to watch Elvis on the Ed Sullivan show. I still enjoy his songs on the "oldies stations." However, I'm not such a fan that I feel compelled to make the pilgrimage to Graceland, like 750,000 people do each year. Nor do I feel any compulsion to become an Elvis impersonator.

Once I was eating lunch at a Po Folks restaurant. In walked an Elvis impersonator. Well, I assumed he was an impersonator and not the real thing. He looked just like Elvis— sideburns, swagger and all, although I don't remember if he was wearing "blue suede shoes." Some Elvis impersonators do a great job; others are poor imitators.

Just wondering: Are our lives good or bad imitations of Jesus? Would anyone ever look at us and see Jesus? These Elvis imitators try to look like, act like and talk like Elvis. Wouldn't it be great if someone said that we reminded them of Jesus because of the way we look, act and talk?

Six Flags Humiliation Park
Some time ago the Davises went with some relatives to the "amusement" park Six Flags. Honestly, I didn't want to go. I went because my son and a nephew and niece were going, and I wanted to appear to be the fun-loving father and uncle. I don't like amusement parks. Why do we call them "amusement" parks anyway? What is so "amusing" about free falling from 200 feet in the air? Heights are not my thing. I like my feet firmly planted on Mother Earth.

Going to Six Flags turned out to be a humiliating experience for me. I'm the person who holds the purses and umbrellas while everyone else rides these terrifying rides. I did agree to accompany my son, niece and nephew on the kiddie roller coaster, The Mine Train. By roller coaster standards, it's a pussycat. The kids loved it. When we exited the ride, Sheri said I was "white as a sheep." Too fast for me. Humiliating.

One area of Six Flags I do enjoy is the game section, where you can shoot basketballs to win prizes, just like the old county fair. After the humiliation of the roller coaster, I thought at least I could gain some respect shooting hoops. Clank. Clank. I tried several shots and drew nothing but iron. Tyler said, "Let me try, Dad." SWISH. Nothing but net. Humiliating.

Finally we all rode Thunder River, an inner tube ride where everybody gets a little wet, but some unlucky soul gets soaking wet because he goes under the waterfall. Guess who? You got it. Every inch of my humiliated soul was drenched. The kids thought it was hilarious.

So what's so "amusing" about getting sick on the kiddie roller coaster, drawing nothing but iron at the basketball goal and getting soaked on Thunder River? Nothing. Humble pie was served, and I ate a big slice.

Humility is a noble and necessary trait for a Christian, and we learn it in various ways. Even an "amusement" park can be a great teacher.

Spud Scud
The Davises arrived at home for Sunday lunch, which constituted of chili in the Crockpot and baked potatoes that had cooked all morning. "Oh no," Sheri exclaimed as she opened the oven door, "a potato exploded." Trying to be cute and add a bit of humor to the situation, I said: "Hmm, I thought I heard a tater ticking." She wasn't amused. Well, I persisted with a follow up one-

liner in hopes of breaking the tension: "What we have is a spud scud." It worked. She smiled. I was secure in my title as house comic.

I've been thinking a lot about that lunch: chili in the Crockpot and spuds in the oven. Each cooked (or simmered) for several hours before being served. One way that people deal with problems or with anger is to stuff it inside. I tend to do that. How about you? It's not the best method. What often happens is that we "stuff" our anger and other feelings for so long that we explode. The explosion is not confined to the oven, unfortunately. Usually, those closest to us, the ones we love the most, are the recipients of our outbursts. When the debris (shrapnel) settles, it's usually on our spouse and children, not because they deserve it, but because they were closest to the explosion. The scriptures say: "Don't let the sun go down upon your wrath." (Ephesians 4:26). In other words, find appropriate ways to express your feelings: pray, cry, talk to a friend, etc. Then perhaps the spud scud will become a dud.

One of Those Days
Have you ever had "one of those days?" Sure you have. Me too. Recently. It started turning sour early with a 9:15 dentist appointment. Need I say more? When a dentist says, "this won't hurt much" my entire body cringes. He pulled out a two foot long needle to "numb" the entire east (or was it west?) side of my mouth. In the process of doing a filling, he had me chomp down and grind my teeth. Several times. Only problem is, one time my tongue got in the way. How would I have known? Couldn't feel it. Mouth was numb. I bit the heck out of my tongue. So, by about 10:15, I'm having

"one of those days." I had one hour before an 11:15 meeting, so I decided to drop by the dry cleaners to pick up some clothes. "Mr. Davis, we've had a problem with one of your suits. There was a pen in the pocket and it exploded, so there is ink all over your suit." (It was my favorite suit.) So it's now about 10:30 and I'm in the middle of "one of those days." What next? I'll go by the house for a moment and take the dry cleaning that is ink-free. When I arrive at home I see the neighbor's dog, Hatfield, roaming around the neighborhood. He has obviously gotten out of their fenced-in backyard. So it's hotter'n Helsinki, but I'm wearing a suit and chasing Hatfield around the neighborhood. So, would you agree that I'm having "one of those days?"

I spent the remainder of the day cringing when the phone rang. What could happen next? I was afraid to listen to the weather report. Hail, tornados, mudslides in Carrollton? I got home late that night after an hour and a half deacons' meeting. "Honey, how was your day?" Sheri asked. "You don't really want to know." At least she didn't quote the Psalmist: "This is the day that the Lord hath made, I will rejoice and be glad in it" (Psalm 118:24). My faith is tested when I have "one of those days." How about you?

Freeing Willy
I saw the movie *Free Willy* a few years ago. The "movie star" was a 9,050 pound killer whale named Keiko. Last week, with the efforts of a Seattle billionaire, the U.S. Air Force and thousands of children around the world, Keiki was hoisted onto a C-17 cargo jet and flown to the freedom of his native waters in Iceland. Keiko will be put in a holding pen, and from

there his handlers hope he will begin socializing with wild killer whales, hone his fish-catching skills, and then after a year or two, go out on his own.

The release effort has touched off controversy about whether a domesticated animal can be returned to the wild. Captive whale specialists have criticized the move, saying Keiko has a slim chance of survival in the cold waters of the North Atlantic after two decades of captivity. They say Keiko would be better off remaining in captivity with other Orcas.

Do you know any Keiko Christians? I do. You know, Christians who are afraid to go out into the cold waters of the real world and relate to others. Do you know people of faith who would rather cloister together than face the daunting challenge of relating to the non-Christian world? Are we willing to socialize with other whales and develop our fish catching skills? Guess what? If we don't, the church will remain in captivity and die. We must leave the safe, secure, guarded waters of the aquarium and swim in the rough seas of a non-Christian society.

"And This Little Piggy Went to…"
By now all are aware of the pigs that have gotten loose in Carrollton and are wreaking havoc in gardens, flowers, etc., around town. Our own James Watkins made the front page of the *Times-Georgian* when the hog herd rambled through his back yard. Some of the pigs have been captured and have gone to the pen—no parole. I know at least one is still on the loose. I know because we saw it. Last Saturday the Davises were having breakfast at the Waffle House on Bankhead

Highway. Dodging traffic like a halfback carrying the "pigskin," America's Most Wanted Pig crossed Bankhead away from the Waffle House. Smart sow. Would you hang around a place that serves fresh ham, bacon and sausage if you were a pig? After its safe pilgrimage across the highway, it ran in the direction of the Ford dealership. Sheri and I speculated that it really was looking for the Pontiac dealership because they sell Trans(H)ams. It probably settled for a Ford Pig-Up.

So, enough of this nonsense. What's the moral of the story, the "pig point," "sow sermon" or "hog homily?"

Our true story reminds me of the chicken and the pig who walked past the Waffle House and saw the sign in the window advertising "Ham and Eggs." The pig said to the chicken, "For you it takes commitment, but for me it's a real sacrifice."

In Hog Heaven

Discovery
How about that John Glenn fellow? Exciting stuff for a seventy-seven year old. Heck, to go up in a spacecraft would be a "high" for any age. I have been thrilled and I'm sure you have at the Discovery's (great name for a spacecraft and a theological journey) recent trip into outer space, made even more exciting by Senator Glenn's presence. I noted with interest his comments from the heavens. The life-long Presbyterian said the view "just strengthens my faith."

"To look out at this kind of creation and not believe in God is, to me, impossible," he said. Amen. Senator

Glenn's argument for the existence of God is a "natural" one, i.e., we can see God in nature. True. We "see" God in a sunrise, sunset, snowfall, etc. However, nature can be evil at times (e.g., hurricanes, floods, droughts) and so what it tells us about God is incomplete.

What Christians believe is that the ultimate picture of what God is like is not snapped from outer space but rather from the foot of the cross. If you really want to know what God is like, become a disciple, not an astronaut. When we follow Jesus, we learn about the God who made the "heavens and the earth." Our Savior came from "the heavens" to reveal to us what God is like; we call it the Incarnation and celebrate it every Christmas. Thank Goodness we don't have to "lift off" in a spacecraft to find God. Our "Discovery" mission can take place any time. "Five, four, three, two, one...Lift off." Are you ready?

Out of Step
I've gotten a good laugh out of it. If you saw Friday's *Times Georgian* then perhaps you have too. The irony was hard to miss. There was a picture in the paper taken at the ARC (Association for Retarded Citizens) dance, and it included yours truly, Mrs. yours truly, Frances Estes and a few others. That's right, DANCE. For a Baptist preacher to have his picture taken at a dance is risky enough. Blackmail is always a possibility. But for it to wind up in the local paper for all my parishioners to see. My, my.

I met a lady one time who was a total stranger, and when I told her I was a Baptist, she said, "Oh, you're the ones who don't dance." "We dance, just not well," I said.

"Lack of practice." When I was growing up in the Baptist Church we were warned against the evils of dancing. Evil thoughts could enter your mind on the dance floor. No one who has ever seen me dance has had an evil thought. Laughing too hard. I never understood why my home church was so against dancing and so for hayrides. Young people could get into more trouble on a long hayride than the adults ever imagined. When the adults asked where we wanted to go on the hayride, we said "Chicago. Drive slowly." Who needs dances when you have hayrides?

The ARC dance was lots of fun and for a very worthy cause. I saw about half the church there. I was tempted to pass the plates and take up an offering. We can't cloister ourselves inside the four walls of the church and never get out into the real world, now can we? Sure there are temptations lurking everywhere: dances, school, work and play. I don't know if Jesus ever went to dances, but he never shied away from mixing it up with sinners. How can you and I ever be "salt and light" unless we do the same?

Nun News

Good Housekeeping is not a magazine that I normally read, but while waiting on some car repairs, I decided to peruse it. I came across an intriguing article about a lady named Dolores Hart. Ms. Hart appeared in eleven movies back in the 50's and 60's, including *King Creole* (1959), *Where the Boys Are* (1960) and *Loving You* (1957). Two of the movies starred Elvis Presley. Dolores and Elvis struck up a friendship. Nothing more, she says. Needless to say, she had a bright acting future, and the sky was the limit for young Dolores Hart. But her life took a different turn. While engaged to a man named Don Robinson, she began to feel that God might be calling her to something else. After much soul searching, she broke off the engagement and told her fiancé that God was calling her to be a nun. That was 1963. Mother Dolores, as she is known, has been at a small abbey in Connecticut ever since. She has spent her years working at various jobs including farming, baking and building cabinets. "I could have had a more lucrative career," she said, "but just how many pairs of shoes can you own? How many cars? How many houses? I always had a need to find a center in which I could offer some ray of hope."

What a good word. Let's pray that we can all find Christ as that "ray of hope."

Gospel Grammar
Having an English literature professor in the congregation makes the pastor nervous. Don't get me wrong. I wouldn't trade Sonja Bagby (and Bob and Joel) for all the tea in China. They're great people. But I'm always afraid that I might slip up grammatically, e.g. lie or lay, swam or swum. When Sheri and I heard about the Grammar Hotline, sponsored by the Writing Center at the University of West Georgia, we were humored by the possibilities. What if all hotlines were connected? Say someone calls 911 and says, "My house <u>are</u> on fire." The operator says, "Your house <u>is</u> on fire." "I know it <u>are</u>, that's why I called you." "Yes sir, but before we send the fire trucks, I'll put you through to the Grammar Hotline." That reminds me of the little boy who went to school and said, "I et six eggs for breakfast this morning." The teacher responds: "You mean ate,

don't you?" Boy to teacher, "Maybe it was eight eggs I et."

I know the rules of grammar, but I suppose that I never get them all right. For instance, I know that a preposition is not something you should end a sentence "with." I also know that we shouldn't split our infinitives but I forget when I'm exhorting the congregation "to" truly "believe."

I know the grammar rules but don't get them right. Some I violate wittingly and others accidentally. Rules are good, and we need some or else we'd all talk like Jed Clampett. They provide guidelines for us and ultimately are for our own good.

Being sinners, we need some rules. However, obsession with the rules for grammar or life will do us no good. If I lived in fear of breaking a grammatical rule, I'd never open my mouth. Conversely, fear of breaking God's laws will turn us into legalistic Pharisees.

We are free in the Spirit. Free from the law. Free to serve Christ. That "are" the truth.

Heaven Can Wait
One week out of the year is National Dog Week. (Should we send cards or flowers?) The theme for the week is "Dog Ownership: A Joyful Lifetime-Rewarding Responsibility." That's a mouthful, but true. Joyful? Usually. Rewarding? Always.

We have a dog, "D.D." She's a wonderful pet and very smart. She will "sit," "shake" and "hug." I'm trying to teach her about computers so she can e-mail her friends. Whoever said that a dog is "man's best friend" was right. She greets me when I come home with a bark and a wagging tail. She wants to play.

I've had lots of dogs in my lifetime: Cessna, Sport, Junior, Tully Babb and Bama. They've all gone the way of Puppy Paradise. Each was special and missed greatly after his or her demise. A children's movie a few years ago was entitled *All Dogs Go to Heaven.* I sure hope so. But what does that title say about our view of the afterlife? Our critics say that Heaven is just wishful thinking. Heaven is described in the Bible as a wonderful place with streets paved of gold, a place where there will be no more suffering or tears. But remember, we have plenty of work to do here. So let's not wish our lives away. God will take care of the future. Live your life in the "here and now" and trust God for the "by and by." Instead of singing "When the Roll is Called Up Yonder," how about a verse or two of "When the Roll is Called Down Here."

Wanted: Dead or Alive
Our dog likes to bark. She barks at the wind. Snails. Birds. Anything that moves, except people. She loves people. She has many different barks. There's the bark at the back door that says, "Come feed me." Then there is the bark at other dogs, which she hates. And of course the bark at things, like snails and birds. A few nights ago we heard a different kind of bark. It was loud, angry, anxious and unrelenting. We turned on the backyard floodlights and discovered that she had an opossum cornered. Guess what the opossum was doing? Playing opossum. No movement. As still as pond

water. It acted like it was dead for several minutes. (I've seen that look on Sunday morning at 11:00 during the sermon.) We put our dog in the garage to bring, hopefully, an end to the chaos. After several minutes of silence, the opossum raised its head, looked around to see if the coast was clear, then scampered off into the night.

Isn't there a lot of opossum playing in ecclesiastical backyards? Maybe we should turn on the floodlights and bring out the barking dogs. Let us never pretend we are something that we're not. Cynics call it hypocrisy. If we're alive in Christ, then let's live like it. Churches are healthy when we are honest about who we are. When what you see is what you get. Opossums play dead when they're actually alive. The only thing worse is playing like we're alive when we're really spiritually dead.

Life Lines
O.K., I admit it. Will you? I watch the ABC TV show, *Who Wants to be a Millionaire?* Not only do I watch it, but I like it. In fact, we watch it as a family. What is it that attracts us? Is it that people like us have a chance to win a million bucks or do we simply enjoy trying to answer the questions? Both, I suppose. The first person to win a million was an IRS agent. He had to use a "Life Line" to call a friend for one of the answers. (Since when does an IRS agent have a friend?) I'm glad he won. Wish I had. Who wants to be a millionaire? I do. Don't you?

The show seems to appeal to some of our worst instincts. Three of the Seven Deadly Sins are Lust,

Envy and Greed. Lust is *wanting* what is not yours. Envy is *wanting* to be like your neighbor. Greed is *wanting* too much. See the common theme? *WANTING.* We spend much of our lives wanting what we can't have. And then, if by chance, (one in a million) we get it, we find it doesn't satisfy. I've read lots of interviews with people who have won the lottery. (I don't play the lottery, by the way.) Many have described the misery that has come from winning. Everybody you've ever known wants a piece of the pie. Family members squabble over it. You quickly find that winning the lottery is not all it's cracked up to be.

Jesus said: "Beware, and be on your guard against every form of greed; for not even when one has an abundance does his life consist of his possessions" (Luke 12:15).

So, "Who wants to be a Christian?"

Love in Any Language
I spent three days at a Pastor's Conference in Florida. It was a tough assignment with weather in the 60's but somebody … The purpose of a Pastor's Conference is to equip ministerial types to be better pastors. Shall we say "the jury is still out" as to its effectiveness with me. I had a great time and actually learned a little bit about theology and sermonizing in between times of goofing off with old friends and playing golf.

My greatest lesson, however, came on the flight home. Seated comfortably on a 777 jet, I noticed immediately that I was surrounded by people of varying nationalities and color. A young black male was seated next to me. He was returning home after an interview for a job with

IBM in Orlando. Seated to my right were two men who were speaking French. I haven't a clue what they were saying 'cause my French ain't that good. Behind me were a couple speaking in another "unknown tongue."

On this particular plane there was a miniature TV screen on the back of every seat. So, all I had to do was take the remote control, program the tiny screen, and I could watch a video. Guess what? It came in four languages. I picked English.

I couldn't help but think of Pentecost, where Simon Peter preached (Acts 2) and the people, who were gathered from all over the world, heard his words in their "own tongue." Technology now does what it took a miracle to do then, hear in a different language. It is now so easy to put the gospel in a language that people understand.

One language that all can understand is that of LOVE. The French, Chinese, German, Spanish, or the neighbor next door, all know it when they hear it. Share it.

Hooked
I'm not the addictive type. Never been hooked on drugs, alcohol or tobacco. Some people have addictive personalities, which means they have a tendency to get hooked on certain things. People in our society have lots of addictive choices: drugs, alcohol, tobacco, sex, sports, Nintendo games, work, food (chocolate milk shakes) and TV. Like I said, I'm not the addictive type but ... I'm hooked. Hooked on *Who Wants to be a Millionaire?* "Sheri, where are we going to dinner?" "McDonalds," she says. "Is that your final answer?" I

ask. Whenever I have a "senior moment" and can't remember something, I use one of my Life Lines. Regis is like one of the family. Sheri thinks I've gone too far with the Regis poster in the bedroom and the "Regis for President" bumper sticker. I mean I absolutely love that show. I may have to go to a Regis Rehab Center to get "unhooked."

There are so many extremes in our world. There are political candidates who are extremist and religious groups as well. Whatever happened to moderation? Isn't that still a good word? Don't we need moderation in most (or all) the things we do? Food? Possessions? Regis? The biblical word is temperance or self-control. In the *Wizard of Id* comic strip, the preacher's sermon is on moderation. On and on the preacher went about temperance in eating, drinking, sleeping, working and playing. After the service someone passed by the preacher in the foyer, shook his hand and said: "I think you overdid it."

Seniors: '70
Someone has defined "mixed emotions" as 1) when your mother-in-law drives your new BMW off a cliff, or 2) when your teenage daughter comes home at 3:00 a.m. with a Gideon Bible in her hand. I've got a third definition: going to your 30th high school reunion. This past weekend proved to contain lots of emotion for me, good and bad, high and low. By the time you make it to your 30th, lots has happened to the ole classmates. Some looked old as dirt. Some looked great. Phyllis looked like she could still be a cheerleader. She has six grandkids. One of my friends remarked: "Maybe I'm

just getting older, but I don't remember my grandmother looking like that."

It was great to see the old gang. Sly was there. Banker. Lives in Dothan. Jacquie Sue lives in Spain. Teaches English at the University of Barcelona. Roger and Danny, who along with "yours truly" made up The Three Musketeers, were there and reminiscing along with "Wormy" (me). All had a great weekend. But it was bittersweet. Two of my namesakes (Davis) have died: Nita and Phil. Homeroom pals. Nice people. And two of my classmates have died of AIDS. Each class reunion I attend reminds me of our two classmates, Michael and Linda, who died in separate accidents during our senior year. DHS Seniors '70 suffered together through the deaths of friends, a 1-9 football season and the struggles of integration. But all of that is balanced by the good times that we shared.

Such is life. It really is a mixed bag. The apostle Paul admonished the Christians in Rome to "weep with those who weep and rejoice with those who rejoice" (12:15). I did a little bit of both this past weekend.

Halfway Herb
Jesus said: "For which of you, desiring to build a tower does not first sit down and count the cost, whether he has enough to complete it?" (Luke 14:28). Good advice for building or entering a parade. In case you've been on another planet and haven't heard, at a recent 4th of July parade, Herb Smith entered his John Deere tractor, pulling a flatbed trailer. Herb serves as Chairman of the West Georgia Two-Cylinder Club and graciously enters a tractor in the parade every year. He delights some

youngsters at the same time. Several children were riding on it, including Taylor, Katherine and Carter Smith, and our son Tyler. All aboard were having a blast, waving at friends and throwing candy, when the tractor/trailer suddenly stopped at the town square. Why? Was Herb asking for directions? Did the kids need a potty break? Floats and tractors don't just stop dead in their tracks in the middle of a parade unless ... they're out of gas! That's right. OUT OF GAS! Herb, the F stands for "full" and the E stands for "empty," and when the arrow is on the E then it's time to fill'r up. Being the resourceful man that he is, Herb decided to coast backwards, downhill, into a gas station. This tale has a happy ending as the tank was filled and Herb and company completed the parade.

The march for freedom is far from complete. As long as people in other countries don't have the right to vote, speak or worship, then freedom's parade is incomplete. As long as people in America fail to honor, cherish and fight for freedom, then our freedoms are endangered. Let us not get halfway home in freedom's march and give out of gas. Our forefathers gave their heart and soul, and sometimes their lives, for religious freedom. Don't quit on them now. Refill your tanks. Finish the course. Thanks, Herb, for the reminder.

P.S. The love offering Sunday morning is for Herb's gas money.

Plain Jane
Forty-six years with one name is a long time. Old habits are hard to break, and I'm kind o' hooked on the old name. Why change it now after forty-six years? It's

like calling your wife of half a century "sugar" when you've been calling her "honey" all these years.

Well, the M&M Company has done it. The Plain M&M's are being renamed Milk Chocolate M&M's. In 1954, the M&M company gave them the "plain" name to distinguish them from the newly introduced peanut M&M's. Recently, the company began a $10 million ad campaign: "Same great chocolate. Much better name." A spokesman for the company said: "For a long, long time, our chocolate has been too good to be called plain …." A spokesman said that calling their candies plain "never really fit the eating experience of M&M's."

I hate to be the one to break the news to the spokesman, but I've eaten about 10 billion M&M's in my lifetime, and I've never found it to be an "eating experience." Eating a rib eye, boiled shrimp, or mama's mashed tater's, now those are eating experiences.

What's wrong with plain anyway? In a Baskin-Robbins world full of Rocky Road, Cookies 'n Cream and Mint Chocolate, what's wrong with a little Vanilla every now and then? Plain o' Vanilla. Does "plain" imply boring, dull, average, and mediocre? What's so wrong with that? Our lives are filled with too many frills and too much entertainment.

We need a little dose of plain. How about plain o' faith? Plain o' walk in the park? Plain o' family prayer time? Sounds good to me. "The Lord preserves the simple" (Psalm 116:6).

Blue Light Special

I recently took Tyler and two of his friends (Michael Hollis and Chase Alford) over to Callaway Gardens to watch the professional golf tournament. Had a great time. The boys spent most of the time over and back talking about the 50% of the world's population that they can't stand—girls. They sure talked a lot about the opposite sex in spite of their disdain for them. On the return trip the boys were horsing around in the backseat, buckled up in their seatbelts, of course. Normal kid stuff. Chase made a list of girls Tyler likes. Michael teased. Tyler had Michael in a headlock. Like I said, normal kid stuff.

I looked in the rearview mirror. Blue light flashing. A police officer was pulling us over. I immediately wondered if the car tag was expired. Couldn't be. Speeding? No way. Was it my theft of bubble gum as a child? College prank catching up with me?

"Officer, what is it?" I asked. "The boys," she said, "are they buckled in? They sure were horsing around in the back seat." The backseat got as quiet as a morgue. "Not a creature was stirring, not even a mouse." Could have heard a pin drop. Eyes as big as silver dollars. Fear. Angst on their faces. That's the quickest way I've ever seen to silence three young boys.

I'm glad to see that all three still have great respect for law officers ... and a little fear. Hopefully all of us still respect people because of their position—mayor, governor, pastor, and teacher. The writer of Proverbs says that respect (fear) of the Lord is the beginning of wisdom (1:7). I suspect that respect for a law officer has made these boys very, very wise.

Cow Copies

To me, a cow is a cow is a cow. With apologies to our own Bill Reynolds, I don't know the difference in a Holstein, Jersey or Hereford. They're all moo cows to me. But Mandy is one of a kind. Mandy is a champion Holstein cow who was auctioned recently as the first farm animal to be cloned for commercial sale. Several calf clones are growing in the wombs of surrogate cattle and they are expected to fetch $50,000 to $100,000 at an auction in Madison, Wisconsin, home of the dairy industry's biggest trade show. Though cattle embryos have been cloned before, no one has made an exact duplicate of an adult cow and sold it. Mandy, age 8, is old by cattle standards, a senior citizen. She produces about 3,300 gallons of milk a year (about the amount that the Davises drink.) Mandy's owner, Ron Bader, was skeptical of cloning when he was approached by a company about making a Mandy copy. But he decided to go ahead with it and said: "You get an exact duplicate. That was what impressed me."

Wouldn't it be great if we could clone Christians? Not that we should all look alike or think alike. I'm not into "cookie cutter" Christians. But we all want to be like Jesus. Exact duplicates of Jesus are what we're after. But true discipleship isn't as easy as cloning. We must pay a price to imitate Jesus. Following after Christ involves a cross, not a clone.

Mail Message

When I was a kid, I went to the movies (picture show as we used to call them) and the previews of upcoming movies were shown. I remember one time when a preview of an upcoming Elvis movie was shown and girls began to scream hysterically. It was just a preview, for Heaven's sake! The girls just loved Elvis the Pelvis. He once recorded a song called "Return to Sender." In it he sings about sending a letter to a girl and the letter kept coming back. "She wrote upon it: Return to Sender," Elvis pined. (Truth is, no girl that I knew would have sent Elvis' letter back.) Anyway, as a kid I became familiar with that phrase "Return to Sender."

I saw it again in Sunday's paper in an article that discussed the U.S. Postal Service's rate hike. Stamps are going up from 33¢ to 34¢. (Still seems like a great deal to me. For 34¢ would you take a letter across the street? Probably not.) So, what do you do if you own a bunch of 33¢ stamps? Buy a bunch of 1¢ stamps to partner with them. Guess what will happen if you mail a letter with a 33¢ stamp? Return to Sender.

I'm sure glad that our messages to God are never "returned" because of insufficient postage. We believe that God always hears our prayers. Always. We may not fully understand the answer to them, but they never return unopened.

We have many great prayer warriors in our congregation. And like the Postal Service, they deliver. Thanks.

"The Colonel Would Roll Over in . . ."
Is it the greatest discovery since the Dead Sea Scrolls or is it a hoax? I'm speaking of the recent finding in Shelbyville, Kentucky. A handwritten note that was found in the basement of a home once owned by Kentucky Fried Chicken founder Colonel Harland

Sanders has sparked quite a controversy. Restaurateurs Tommy and Cherry Settle, who bought the home in the 1970's, found the note in their basement in a leather-bound date book from 1964. Tommy Settle was "licking his fingers" over the prospects of authenticating the recipe and selling the book to a collector. KFC cried "fowl" and responded with a lawsuit (i.e., we'll "wring your neck"). KFC officials told Mr. Settle not to "count his chickens before they hatch," adamantly maintaining that this was not the Colonel's original secret blend of 11 herbs and spices.

That story reminds me of an Old Testament one. Young King Josiah (II Kings 22) was having the Temple renovated when the priest Hilkiah discovered a "Book of the Law." Many scholars think it was a lost copy of a portion of Deuteronomy. When Josiah read it to the people, a national revival ensued. Apparently, the people were "starving" for more than chicken.

We Baptists laugh about all the fried chicken we eat. In fact, I've heard it referred to as the Gospel Bird. Josiah found that people had a hunger for things much deeper than anything the Colonel could cook up. In each person is a heart-shaped vacuum that only God can fill. Now there's a recipe that will "fly." The secret is out!

"As the heart panteth after the water brooks, so panteth my soul after thee, O God" (Psalm 42:1).

Stuff
I discovered these two seemingly unrelated newspaper items on the same day. In one, scientists poring over the almost completed map of human DNA reported renewed

confirmation of the unity of the human race, gender or nationality. Based on DNA from both sexes and from persons of Africa, Asian, Hispanic and European descent, each person shares 99.99 percent of his or her genetic code with all others. In other words, beneath our skin, we're all very much alike.

The other article reported that two firefighters sifting through a partially burned-out house in Atlanta's West End neighborhood discovered about $200,000 in cash. The house belonged to Robert Elmo Sharpton, who died last April at the age of 74. It turns out that Sharpton's bank account and stocks are worth about $6.7 million, though he lived like a miser. Neighbors described him as kind but incredibly frugal. "Never saw him with a new pair of shoes," said one neighbor. Sharpton never married and had no children, but a judge ruled that his 78-year-old girlfriend was his common-law wife and legal heir. "I guess he thought he was going to live forever," said a cousin, "and maybe take it with him when he went."

Two stories about stuff. One about the stuff we're made of and the second what we make with our stuff. Jesus said, "Where the heart is there will your treasure be also" (Matt. 6:21). We're all not alike. Some have generous hearts. Others are misers. Some hoard their stuff. Others share it.

Pulpits and Steeples
I remember when I was a kid being in awe of pulpits. The preacher who stood behind it was bigger than life, and the pulpit itself was a holy piece of furniture. And then came the day when I actually looked inside one.

Not what I had expected to see: paper clips, Butterfinger wrappers, months-old Communion cups and last week's children's sermon. In a similar vein, the recent lightning strike at our church has necessitated the cleaning out of our steeple. (Actually, the fire chief strongly suggested it.) So, some brave young men in our church climbed up into the sacred steeple. On the outside it's a beautiful brick steeple that points to the heavens. Not so on the inside. You wouldn't believe the junk that came out of that religious edifice: dust, light bulbs, audio speakers and bird carcasses. So far they have not uncovered the Ark of the Covenant, the bones of former pastors, deacons, or Jimmy Hoffa.

Steeples (and pulpits) are symbolic of the people who worship beneath them. We're a lot prettier on the outside than on the inside. And cleaning up our insides is an ongoing process that must be intentional and deliberate. Sometimes the preacher (or fire chief) suggests it, and at other times the storms of life (lightning) precipitate it. But it must be done. Not periodically, but daily. Jesus said, "For out of the heart come evil intentions, murder, adultery, fornication, false witness, slander" (Matthew 15:19). Clean it up!

Toll Theology

Florida officials say that Wesley Ridgewell is guilty of zipping through 705 tollbooths without paying and thus is one of the state's biggest toll thieves. They allege that during 1999-2000, automatic cameras took 705 photos of his late model Honda with his license plate "JST CRZY." Ridgewell disputes the claims, saying someone stole one of his license plates and put it on a similar car. Law enforcement officials, however, feel like they have

Steeple People

the right guy in spite of his protests. "I'm such a good person. People who know me just can't believe this is happening." He is facing up to $15,000 in fines instead of a quarter here and 50 cents there in tolls.

His protest of innocence sounds like a lot of people I've come across in my lifetime. We all must pay a toll. Life demands it. Daily. A quarter here and there. Often more. Sometimes we pay dearly for the right of passage onto certain of life's highways. None of life's journeys come without a price. If you try to cheat life, then you pay later. Jesus said that if we follow him we must first "count the cost" (Luke 14:28). How much? Surely a little bit every day and a lot over a lifetime. So, don't cheat the tollbooth. Pay now or you'll pay dearly later.

Lookout
If you grew up in the South, you know about Ruby Falls, Rock City and Lookout Mountain. They say that from Lookout Mountain one can see seven states: Tennessee, Georgia, Alabama, North Carolina, South Carolina, Virginia and Kentucky. I went when I was a kid. Been so long ago I think some of the states were colonies. Instead of saying that one can see seven states, they should advertise six states and paradise (Alabama). Well, we've been to Chattanooga a few times in recent years, having seen the Aquarium and other tourist attractions and, of course, we've seen the signs for Lookout Mountain. This past weekend on our trip to Nashville, we passed through that "neck of the woods" again, but this time I noticed another sign. Right next to the one for Lookout Mountain was another, Lookout Valley. My mind immediately went into ministerial fifth gear. If one can see seven states from Lookout

69

Mountain, what can one see from Lookout Valley? Truth is, we learn more and see more in the valleys of life then the mountains. C.S. Lewis said God whispers to us in our joy but shouts to us in our pain. Valleys are tough. Valleys are necessary. Valleys sharpen our vision.

Are you in a valley? Stay focused. What can you see? Seven states. The State of Peace, Patience, Kindness, Humility, Dependence, Repentance and Contentment. What a view!

Signs and Wonders?
It was the headline that caught my attention: "Man Shot to Death in Shadow of Ten Commandments Sign." The story goes like this. Circuit Judge Mac Parsons of Birmingham recently put up a sign listing the commandments in the New Hill community on the west side of that city. Having grown tired of seeing murder cases from the community in his court, he posted the commandments and highlighted "Thou shalt not kill." The sign failed. Within five hours, the sign had been knocked over and a young man had been shot to death a block away. Said the judge: "When people are selling drugs, burning down houses and committing murder, I think they need exposure to the Ten Commandments." He went on to say that placing the commandments in high crime communities "would benefit a lot more people than putting them up for a bunch of lawyers, judges and bureaucrats." He was, of course, referring to the recent debate about displaying them in courthouses.

I certainly like the judge's spirit and attitude and I, in fact, agree with his logic. I also admire his missionary spirit. I wonder, however, if the apostle Paul would look favorably on the posting of the Law. He knew all the laws, but until he met Christ, he could never keep them. Paul could quote the Ten Commandments and hundreds more, backwards and forwards, but it did no good until that day on the Damascus Road.

Face it, we're not going to change the world by posting commandments or by flexing our political muscle. "Not by might, nor by power," saith the Lord, "but by my spirit" (Zechariah 4:6).

Literal Language
Interpreting scripture can be difficult at best. We look at certain passages and wonder "literal" or "figurative?" Compounding the difficulty is our misunderstanding of language. We seem not to understand the meaning of literal. A football player once said after winning a big game, his team was "literally on cloud nine." A basketball coach was quoted as saying after a tough loss, "We literally fell apart tonight." Another coach whose team had a lot of injuries said, "We're literally held together by tape." Then another coach after a huge upset victory said, "I was literally beside myself." (Wouldn't that look funny?) What all of these well-intentioned but grammatically-flawed people meant was "figurative" not "literal." When someone is "literally scared to death," then they are dead. Call the funeral home. What they mean is figurative.

Much in the Bible is to be taken literally: "As they were coming down the mountain, Jesus ordered them ..." (Matthew 17:9). Much in the Bible is to be taken figuratively: "It is easier for a camel to go through the eye of a needle than for a rich man to enter the kingdom" (Matthew 19:24).

The bumper sticker that says, "The Bible says it, I believe it, that settles it" has never settled it for me. I must look at each passage seriously to determine, among other things, is it "literal" or is it "figurative." A Baptist leader once said that Jesus was speaking "literally figurative" when describing the bread and wine as His body and blood. Huh?

The Bible is chock-full of poetry, prose, parables, riddles, etc. Each type of literature demands careful attention and our best hermeneutical (interpretive) skills, guided by God's spirit. In doing such, we honor the Bible, God's holy word.

Party Time
Hope you had a good New Year's Eve. We did. Hung out with friends. Kind of subdued. We were in Alabama, which is in Central Time. We decided that since their midnight would be 1:00 a.m. for our body-clocks (Georgia time), we celebrated the New Year at 11:00 p.m. We watched Dick Clark on TV (whoopie do) and drank Cokes to celebrate. It wasn't exactly a wild and crazy party. Believe me, there is nothing like partying with a "man of the cloth." The only hangover we had the next day was from an overdose of football.

I read an interesting article about how to feel better if one does have a hangover from too much alcohol. Believe it or not, the old favorite, coffee, does get the medical thumbs-up. Too much alcohol widens the blood vessels, whereas the caffeine in coffee works as a vasoconstrictor, closing the vessels. There are other solutions, such as Puri Tea, which increases kidney function and improves liver function, which of course, helps to purify the body. Bridgette Mars, the creator of Puri Tea, said her goal was to create a tea that would remove toxins from the body, not to enable people to get drunk more often. Then she said: "A hangover might really be a blessing. It will teach you not to do that too often."

Bridgette, I'm not so sure that the misery of a hangover is a really good deterrent to excessive drinking. It does raise the question, though, of what motivates people to change their behavior. Fear of negative consequences may not be the most effective motivator. I would rather stress the positive. Following Christ as serious disciples has changed millions of lives. Jesus can change you and me. "Be not drunk with wine wherein is excess, but be filled with the Spirit" (Ephesians 5:18).

Peggy's Pulpit
I'll never forget the first time I heard the song. It stopped me in my tracks. "Is That All There Is?" was its title. Its singer was Peggy Lee. She died recently at the age of 81 after a "long and illustrious" career as a singer, (700 recordings and 59 albums), songwriter and actress. Critics said her voice was "sultry." It was like you were alone with her when she sang. Pillow talk. "Peggy Lee sends her feelings down the quiet center of her notes," said one critic.

Peggy Lee had a rough childhood, losing her mother when she was four and being abused by her stepmother. Perhaps those experiences spilled over into her songs, especially "Is That All There Is?" The song is tragic. It depicts a little girl who experiences things like the circus. After each experience, Peggy Lee sings the chorus: "Is that all there is, my friend? If that's all there is, then let's keep dancing, let's bring out the booze and have a ball, if that's all there is."

I feel terribly sorry for people who are so bored with life that pleasurable experiences have no meaning. People like that have lost zest for life; the well of life has run dry. How tragic.

As Christian people, we have a purpose in living. Our commitment to Christ gives meaning to things that otherwise might be empty. God has a purpose for us— a reason for our being.

So, "Is That All There Is?" No. There is more, so much more, when Christ is in our lives.

Disciplined Driving
I was passed on the highway recently by a lady who was driving at least 50 mph while putting on her make-up. Steering was done by her knees, I assume. Not only was she endangering others on the road, but I think she mistakenly put some rouge down her ear canal.

Speaking of distractions, a study was conducted of accidents caused by driver distractions. The research rated common foods eaten in cars, based on the degree of distraction while eating with only one hand on the wheel. The top ten from bad to worse: (10) chocolate (9) soft drinks (8) jelly and cream-filled donuts (7) fried chicken (6) barbecue (5) hamburgers (4) chili (3) tacos

(2) hot soups and #1? Coffee. Unexpected splashes and spills. Then the driver tries to clean up while driving and winds up in the proverbial ditch. No big surprises on the list, though I might have found a spot for boiled peanuts. Tough to shell them and then dispose of the hulls while harmonizing with your latest Garth Brooks CD.

Distractions. The writer of Hebrews had a word or two to say about those. Chapter 12:1-2 reads: " ... let us run with endurance the race that is set before us, fixing our eyes on Jesus, ... " In other words, focus. Be committed to the task at hand, whether driving or discipleship.

There are many distractions in our society. Life's highway is lined with billboards. Author Charles Poole's dad gave this piece of advice about plowing, which I think applies to driving and living: "Son, when I plow, I look way out to the end of the row and plow to where I'm going, ... "[2]

Baptismal Blues

I've known some preachers who were a "stick in the mud." Never thought I would be one. But, our recent outdoor baptism proved me wrong. Surely you have heard by now. Your minister got stuck in the lake. Literally. Those darn waders sank about one foot in the sand and muck. Someone took pictures to prove it. I was so deep in the sand it looked like David baptizing Goliath. Danny DeVito in a baptismal robe. I did the four baptisms and all was well until I tried to exit the

---

[2] Charles E. Poole, *The Tug of Home; Restful Words For Weary Families* (Peake Road, 1997) 34.

lake. Couldn't move. Left leg. Stuck. Right leg. Stuck. I'm dead serious. Stuck like a tattoo on Dennis Rodman. A song came to mind: "I was sinking deep in sin (or was it sand), far from the peaceful shore." By the way, I pastored a church one time that would have left me out there. In fact, they would have gone straight to the house and formed a Pulpit Committee to search for a new pastor. Thank goodness, some kind souls in our church "bailed me out."

Have you ever been spiritually stuck? I have been. How about you? Are your prayers hollow? Is your soul drained? For us to grow in faith, we need new challenges that will stretch us. We need new commitments that will force us to tackle the disciplines of our faith. And we may need a Christian brother or sister to assist us out of the "sinking sand" and get us on solid ground again. If you find yourself spiritually stuck, then genuine worship and fellowship with other Christians is a great way to find those new challenges and commitments.

Jesse the Baptist
Cemetery workers in Texas recently dug up the remains of a man who died in 1951and who had claimed to be the legendary outlaw Jesse James. History books have said that James was shot and killed by Bob Ford in 1882 in St. Joseph, Missouri. But people in Granbury, Texas, have claimed for years that J. Frank Dalton, who is buried under a gravestone that reads "Jesse Woodson James" with the inscription "Supposedly killed in 1882," is "the" Jesse James. They say James faked his death in 1882 and lived to the ripe old age of 104. A DNA

expert will perform an analysis of the remains to determine the true identity.

What you may not know is that Jesse and his brother, Frank James were PK's, a.k.a. Preacher's Kids. Their father was a Baptist preacher. Ouch. So, is there a Baptist in this tomb? And what would the DNA of a Baptist look like? I think you will find that we Baptists have traditionally come in all shapes and sizes, from varying theologies and worship styles. (I'm not suggesting that most Baptist are outlaws.) Given the Southern Baptist Convention controversy of the past twenty years, the face of Baptists has really changed. We are becoming much more monolithic, i.e., one shape and size fits all. What Baptists have traditionally stood for however, are these principles:

1. Soul Freedom—otherwise known as the priesthood of the believer.
2. Bible Freedom—our freedom to interpret scripture for ourselves, without someone telling us what it means.
3. Church Freedom—local church autonomy— our right to determine our fate ourselves.
4. Religious Freedom—separation of church and state—a free church is a free state.

In the future when people dig up Baptists, what will they find?

D.D. Update
I love our dog, D.D. She is absolutely the greatest dog on the planet. She is cute, playful and smart. Smart? She sits on command (sometimes). Shakes. Gives hugs. E-mails her friends. I recently took her to the vet for a

check-up. It had been too long since I'd taken her, and I knew it. Slightly "guilt ridden" would describe my feelings as we entered the animal hospital. D.D. was the hit of the place. She extended her paw to every person who entered the room, wanting to shakes hands (paws). She shook so many hands I thought she was running for political office. She did everything but kiss babies.

Then the check-up. Needles. Prods. You name it. Then the results. "She looks great except, except ... for heartworms." My heart sank. Heartworms? They can be fatal, can't they? My slightly guilt-ridden self turned into a woeful, remorseful self. I love my dog, but I had failed to give her the heartworm medication because we had run out. You know about good intentions. I meant to get some more. Could'a. Would'a. Should'a. But didn't.

Thankfully, the doctor explained that the illness was detected early, is treatable and D.D. should live to shake hands for several years to come. I picked my guilt-ridden self off the floor and vowed to be a better master to my "best friend."

"To whom much is given, much is expected" (Luke 12:48).

Does it Taste Like Chicken?

If you ever go to Wausau, Florida, you might want to check out the local Possum Festival in this tiny Panhandle town. (No one spells it opossum here.) Local politicians turn out in droves. It has become a key stop on the campaign trail. Said one local congressional candidate, while shaking his head at his fate: "The things you've got to do." What things? Shake hands. Pose with babies. Eat possum. Eat possum? Yep. Said the Agricultural Commissioner: "As wild game goes, it's okay. If you can get the grease off it."

However, eating possum is not for everyone. Tallahassee mayor Scott Maddox said, "There are some things I will not do to garner votes. I won't lie, I won't kowtow to the special interests and I won't eat possum." But, even those who don't eat one of the critters, like Maddox, purchased one at the auction. You see, buying one, getting on stage at the Possum Palace (where the event is held) and holding the thing by the tail, practically ensures a picture in the local paper. Locals say it is very difficult to win an election without an appearance at the Possum Festival. Said local state representative Bev Kilmer, "The local people here judge whether a candidate cares about them by whether they make this a priority."

Hmmm. Eating possum = caring. All of us are called on to do things we don't like doing to symbolize our love and compassion for others. Do you enjoy visiting the hospital? Nursing home? Funeral home? Who said compassion was easy or following Christ would be a piece of cake? Piece of cake or piece of possum? Which will it be?

Deflated
I suppose there is never a good time for a flat tire. However, having one over the holidays with the van parked in the driveway beats having one on a school morning or on a deserted road in the middle of nowhere. So, I'm grateful for small blessings.

It's been awhile since I've changed a flat tire. Piece of cake, I thought. Not so fast, my friend. First, I couldn't find the tire tool and jack. I hate to admit that I had to consult the car manual to discover that it is stored in a side panel. Great. Now all I need is a spare tire. Where could it be? Had to get out the manual once again. You'll never guess where they put spare tires these days. Underneath the car! Now how to retrieve it. After consulting with my brothers (who were visiting for the holidays and who are automotively challenged) for several minutes, I once again read the manual. Are you noticing a pattern here? When in doubt, read the manual.

The last thing in the world a man wants to do (besides stopping to ask for directions) is to read the instructions or consult the manual. We feel like we can figure it out on our own. To read the directions would be an admission of something our wives learned a long time ago—we aren't omniscient.

We'd all make it better, in life and in particular in our spiritual travels, if we'd read God's manual. The Bible has some great instructions for us when life goes flat. Read it.

Technology Retreat
Several months ago our 27" TV went blank. KO'd. Beyond repair. It was the TV in our living room, and the one we watched as a family. Twenty-seven inches is not extremely large as TV's go, but it was the biggest one in our home. We have a smaller one, 13", that we moved into its place. Our intention has been to purchase

a new one, but our old buddy procrastination has taken up residence. Doing without a "large" TV for several months has, quite frankly, been good for us. I've reminded the family of my childhood when we had black and white TV that only received three channels, complete with the antennae that had to be turned in the direction of Montgomery to pick up NBC clearly.

Recently our dishwasher gave up the ghost as well. So, for several days we've made the most of local restaurants, paper plates and the old fashioned "wash them by hand." Again, having to make do without another modern convenience hasn't been all bad.

My pager also bit the dust recently. I suppose that using it as a hockey puck for floor hockey contributed to its demise. So, for several days my pager was out of commission, and I was out of reach. It felt soooo good to know that if people wanted to reach me, they would have to do it the old-fashioned way—the telephone.

I resisted the technology age for several years, but eventually I had to get with the times like everyone else. I'm now armed with computer, pager, cell phone, etc. They do make life easier and make work more efficient. But better? The jury is still out on that. The fact that we did without some of our modern conveniences for a few days or weeks by accident is no feather in the Davis' cap. However, it might do us all some good to make the choice of "stepping back in time" and doing without the TV, pager and other gadgets to slow down, simplify and focus our lives. That's not a bad idea for a thoroughly modern Christian.

Steve Davis

I Walk the Line

I asked Tyler if he had ever heard of Johnny Cash. "No," was his reply. I tried to tell him a little about this legend of country and rock music who died this past week. His friend Kris Kristofferson said that Cash was "a walking contradiction, partly truth and partly fiction." The contradiction is perhaps what made him so popular. He was friends with "presidents, preachers and punks," as someone described him. On the one hand, he professed his Christian faith and appeared on the Billy Graham crusades. On the other hand, he once kicked out the spotlights at the Grand Ole Opry and got caught smuggling amphetamines across the Mexican border. In describing her dad's wild younger years, his daughter, Roseanne, said, "Yes, my dad was crazy. He was the prototypical rock star on the road." Cash's Christian faith came to him indirectly through the tragic death of his brother, Jack, who came out of a coma and spoke of seeing "a beautiful city" with "angels singing." That was the pivotal spiritual experience for Johnny Cash.

Even though his life was in many ways a "walking contradiction," he connected with people—with the average man. One of the reasons he connected so well was his voice. It was distinct and unique and as someone said, "It carried the profound power of believability and dignity." His friend Kris Kristofferson may have put it best: "Johnny Cash's voice is the perfect voice for a man of his spirit. It's unmistakable. It doesn't sound like anybody else. And it sounds like the real thing, which is what he is."

Could it be that we might connect with others if we were more authentic? What if our voice had the sound of believability? None of us are completely pure, and we

82

are all, in a sense, "walking contradictions," because none of us have it together all the time. We fall short of the mark, and we profess one thing and do another. Perhaps we should all adopt the unforgettable opening line from his song "I Walk the Line": "I keep a close watch on his heart of mine."

Excuses
One of comedian Jay Leno's favorite subjects is "dumb crooks." Well, Jay, here is some good comedic material for you. This just in from Miami: Police there have arrested a man who allegedly robbed two banks within twenty minutes and then stopped to rest his tired feet. His name is Daniel Gallagher, 46, and he walked into the banks and told tellers he had a bomb in his bag, but the bomb was, in fact, a can of beer. In both cases he demanded and received $100 from tellers. Gallagher told police that his feet became tired after the second robbery, and so he sat down for a rest. Gallagher, who has an extensive criminal record, told the authorities that he committed the bank robberies because, "I'm too ugly to get a job."

The AP article that I read did not include a picture of Gallagher. Maybe I should be glad about that, but if he is going to use his ugliness as an excuse, I would at least like to judge for myself. Remember the old taunt? "U.G.L.Y, you ain't got no alibi, you're ugly, absolutely ugly." Maybe he is. And it is true that in our culture people who are handsome or pretty seem to be favored for jobs and promotions versus those who aren't. But "too ugly to get a job" sounds like an excuse to rob banks instead of working.

I think some people in our society tend to make excuses for their failures, blaming it on their past, family dysfunction, or societal injustices. With Christ we can overcome whatever hand has been dealt us. Conversely, we should be compassionate towards those who bring a lot of baggage from their past. It is not easy to shake your addictions, demons and psychoses from a troubled history.

But what about Mr. Gallagher's ugliness? Maybe what he needs is a little bit (or a lot) of grooming and a relationship with God.

Love it or "Leave" it
We have 1,562,972 leaves in our yard. I know because I counted them. I'm just glad to report that most of them are now in a big pile at the street. I must confess that raking leaves is not my favorite pastime. It ranks just behind sitting in Atlanta traffic and root canals. Growing up in south Alabama, we raked pine straw instead of leaves; I feel the same way about raking pine straw as I do leaves.

It does amaze me, by the way, that we now pay for pine straw. Yard work in general has never been my favorite thing, though I don't now complain about doing it as much as I did as a kid. Believe me, the Davis boys spent their fair share of time working in the yard. Mom liked to have the prettiest yard in the neighborhood, and we were an integral part of her plans. In fact, I got a monogrammed rake for my sixteenth birthday. I spent so much time in the yard that my friends teased me about it. One time on their way to the beach they made a special trip by my house just to blow the horn, wave and "rub it in."

What precipitated my diligent work in the yard this time was that there is a baby shower at our house this week. (I'm glad to report that the stork is visiting other folk besides the Davises.) This blessed event at our home provided the motivation to beautify the premises. Motivation is what makes the world go round and gets leaves raked. So, what provides your impetus for everyday living? We all need a spark.

Sweet Treat
Knowing that you are all anxious for an '04 update on our wonderful puppy D.D., here goes. Actually this is more of an update on how Natalie and D.D. get along. In a word, wonderfully. There is nothing our daughter would rather do than go to the back door and call the dog. And D.D. comes bounding up the steps of the back porch into the waiting arms and eager, waiting-to-be-licked face, of a one-year-old. And in Natalie's hand is always a doggie treat. Well, recently we let D.D. into the house for a while, and she and Natalie played. Sheri noticed Natalie giving her a treat, but thought nothing of it. Later, as Sheri took D.D. to let her out of the house, Sheri looked into the box of treats and noticed that all ten or so were gone. Natalie had given them all to the dog! That would be like setting ten strawberry shortcakes in front of me and saying, "please eat." "Well, OK, if you twist my arm."

Too much of a good thing. One of the big issues for Christians in our culture is just that. We have a lot of good things, but we have a tendency to overindulge in them. We can understand a dog eating ten treats, but there is no excuse for some of our excesses. "In all things moderation," is a phrase we have heard all of our lives. There is no question that many in our culture (and churches) overindulge in food and entertainment. The recent Super Bowl is perhaps the quintessential example. Yes, I watched it and ate before, during and after the game, not really caring who won. Let me strongly encourage you, for the good of your spiritual health, to seek the path of moderation.

Baby Talk
It's lots of fun watching children grow up. Being an older dad, I am really enjoying it the second time around. I seem to be less stressed, and I am paying attention to the little things that she does. Natalie is now learning lots of new words. "Ball," "more," and "uh oh" are some of her favorites. I'm trying, but to no avail, to teach her to say "scholarship." Every child, early on I suppose, learns to say "uh oh." It's a part of the parents' vocabulary and children quickly pick up on the fact that "uh oh" indicates something unexpected has happened. However, in Natalie's case, she will intentionally drop a toy or as she did one day, throw down her doll, and exclaim "uh oh." At some point in her young life I will try to teach her the difference between deliberate acts and accidents. Life is full of both.

We humans bear the responsibility for our choices. I don't deny the role of genetics (nature) in the shaping of our lives and, in fact, I believe that some of who we are is programmed from birth. I also believe, however, that we must bear ultimate responsibility for our choices and the way we use or don't use the gifts and talents we have inherited since birth. I also believe that we make our own moral and ethical choices, although I acknowledge that our environment shapes us (nurtures) to some degree and some have, from birth, tendencies towards certain behaviors, such as alcohol abuse. All of this should make us compassionate towards others whose environment is not as wholesome as ours is and those whose personality type is also more prone to addictive, self-destructive behavior. So, how much of a person's behavior do we attribute to nature and how much to nurture? I'm not smart enough to answer that one. But biblical truth points to our accountability to God for our actions. We can't go through life saying "uh oh."

Limping
Our lawn mower had an accident. It ran into our van. Or should I say, our van ran into it? Either way, the mower sustained a major injury. One of its four tires, the right front one, was broken. What good is a three-wheeled mower? We checked with K-Mart, Wal-Mart, Home Depot and Lowe's, but to no avail. No one carried that size tire anymore. What to do? Buy a new mower? All the while, the grass in our backyard grew as high as the FBC steeple.

Our three-wheeled mower reminded me of a dog that we had when I was growing up. Her name was Bama. She was one tough Chihuahua. In her last years she was blind in one eye and couldn't see out of the other. She also had an unfortunate collision with a car and lost. She walked with a limp. But she got around. Her courage inspired me to take the injured mower and tackle the knee-high grass. Guess what? You can mow with a three-legged mower. You can. The yard may not look as smooth as when mowed with a healthy mower, but it can be done. My mower now has a name, Bama.

If the truth be known, we all walk with a limp. All of us have been injured by life—some self-inflicted wounds and some imposed on us by others. But believe me, we all have our share of breaks and scars. If you don't, then you haven't lived long enough. And the truth is, we are often much better people with a limp than without it. We are more sensitive, caring and compassionate with our wounds than we are without them. Remember Jacob from the Old Testament? He had an all-night encounter with God and was left with a limp. And he was a better person because of it. So, keep limping and keep mowing.

Oldies

Have you ever just bought something on the spur of the moment? Of course you have. We all have. I don't do a lot of that but occasionally something will catch my eye. Most of the time it is a necktie. Tyler and I went shopping recently for a CD that he wanted. It was a recent hits CD, with a bunch of songs that I don't know. While in the music section I saw one I wanted. It was a collection of number one hits from the 60's. What particularly caught my eye was the song "Honey" by Bobby Goldsboro. You may not know that he was an across-the-street neighbor of mine in Dothan, Alabama, when I was growing up. He was a pretty big star back in the 60's with several hits and his own TV show. "Honey" was his biggest hit. It's a real "tear-jerker." On the way home from the store, I made Tyler listen to it and several other songs off the CD, such as "Hang on Sloopy" and "Monday, Monday." It was the longest ride home of his life. You would have thought I was making him watch an episode of the "Gong Show." "Dad, do you actually like that song?" We all tend to think that the music we grew up with was the greatest. And the current music, whatever it might be, stinks.

All of this points out the gap that exists between generations. I get tired of people always talking about how bad the current generation is and how great things used to be. Will Rogers was right when he said: "Things ain't what they used to be and probably never were." My good old days were the 60's. Good old days? How about three assassinations, race riots, war protests, Kent State killings and bell-bottom pants? Were those times any better than these? I think not. Our country has some great young people it in who are going to make us proud. And so does our church. And by the way, I think today's music is "groovy."

Big Mac Attack
I suppose that commenting on a movie you haven't seen is like commenting on a church service you didn't attend. So, I begin with a disclaimer: I haven't seen the movie. I read a review of it. We may institute a Sunday service review in the newsletter for those who happened to miss it. The movie is *Super-Size Me*, a documentary by and about Morgan Spurlock, who goes on a 30-day McBinge. The rules are that he can eat only at McDonald's, and he must have three meals a day, trying everything on the menu in the month's time. If an employee asks if he wants to super-size his order, he must say yes. Spurlock got the idea for the movie after hearing about two overweight teens who sued McDonald's for making them fat. Though the case was

dropped, Spurlock decided to test the fast-food chain's claim, made during the suit, that its food is nutritious. In four weeks he gained almost 25 pounds, his cholesterol shot up 40 percent and he began to suffer liver problems.

This film offers up some amazing facts: More people worldwide eat at McDonald's daily than the entire population of Spain. Also it claims that one in four people in Mississippi is obese. The movie lets McDonald's off the hook a bit by showing the employees to be friendly and the food, he admits, tastes good. And ultimately, the movie asserts, the responsibility falls on the customer, who makes his choice about what he will eat and thus, about his health.

"In all things moderation" goes the popular saying. Or "too much of anything is a bad thing." Moderation is a Christian virtue. The apostle Paul uses the word temperance to describe one of the fruits of the Spirit (Galatians 5:22). Temperance means self-control or moderation. One who is moderate is not given over to extremes. Being a moderate in eating, exercising, working, playing or in theology (in my opinion) is a good thing. It seems to me that Christians in America have very little moderation, especially when it comes to eating. Instead of "super-sizing," maybe a little "down-sizing" is in order.

Pastor Steve
My senior year of college was two of the best years of my life. I crammed four years of college into five. I was having too much fun to graduate. I did however, spend seven hard years in seminary obtaining two advanced degrees. So, yes, I earned a doctorate but

could care less if you call me Dr. or Reverend. Truthfully, "Pastor Steve" has always been my favorite title from kids. "Pastor" describes my calling and Steve makes it personal.

Having worked hard for my degrees, I read with much interest that eleven Georgia educators had their licenses revoked by the Professional Standards Commission. All eleven—ten teachers and a principal—bought advanced degrees from a university that requires little or no course work. Shame on them. I have noticed that many preacher types like being called "Doctor" when, truthfully, they have never attended seminary and some have not finished college. I've known some ministerial "Doctors" who have mail-order degrees.

Why? Why do they do it, and why do churches hire them? Perhaps some ministers like to hide their insecurities with a title. Churches might want their egos stroked by having a "doctor" in the pulpit. It's an odd thing to say the least. I am disheartened, however, when the state Department of Education seems to have more ethics than some ministers and churches. We shouldn't allow ministers with bogus, mail-order degrees to preach in our pulpits any more than schools should allow such teachers to teach.

The fact that I am writing this article points out the log in my own eye. Arrogance. Those of us with earned doctorates can be awfully snooty towards those who have bogus ones. Which is worse, an earned degree with pride or a bogus one with humility? Woe is me! Paul reminded us in Romans 12:3, "I say to everyone among you not to think of yourself more highly than you ought to think."

The Most Holy Father Right Reverend Doctor Steve

One

Leave it to 60's rock group "Three Dog Night" to inspire the preacher. Their song "One" comes to mind. "One is the loneliest number that you'll ever do." Amen, brother. I was single for years before finally tying the knot. There's certainly nothing wrong with being single if you can handle the alone times. Jesus was single. I was a single adult minister at a church for a brief time, and I tried to guide a large group of singles. When it comes to being single, I know about that which I speak. However, when it comes to being a "single parent" I am among the uninitiated. That is, until this past weekend. Sheri, for the first time, took off with some girl friends on Thursday evening for a couple of days in Florida for some R&R. When she left on Thursday, she had a smile on her face as big as I have seen since I first proposed to her in the parking lot of Crazy Jose's Restaurant in Beaumont, Texas. I don't know if she was smiling so big because of the approaching R&R or because she knew I would be a single parent for a few days. Her smile had a sinister look to it.

Well, while she was snoozing in some Florida hotel, I was up at 3:00, 4:00 and 5:00 a.m. on the first evening. (I don't know for sure what she was doing at that time of the morning, and I'm not about to ask). I cooked breakfast one day—Pop Tarts—and went to Jerry's Country Kitchen the next. I dropped off our son at a birthday party and picked him up later. I changed diapers and picked up puzzles and Play-Doh off the floor. I fed the dog. When my lovely bride returned, I quickly gave her a litany of my accomplishments. She wasn't impressed. "I'm glad you missed me," was her smiling response.

I walked in her shoes for long enough to know they're uncomfortable at times. Maybe we should all change roles from time to time that we might be more compassionate, understanding, and helpful to one another. Jesus accepted the ultimate role-reversal in becoming human and "walking among us." He celebrated, hungered, grieved, prayed, befriended, and died—not only as God, but as human. And it is Jesus who said, "Judge not that you not be judged." Walking in another's shoes helps us to love as Christ loves and to minister to real needs with a first hand perspective.

Steve, Size 9½ D

Clichés

The sports world is loaded with cliches, such as "I gave 110%" (which, by the way, is impossible to do), "take it one game at a time" (how else could you take it?) and "it ain't over till it's over" (brought to you by the Department of Redundancy Department). Well, there is a new cliché, and we might as well get used to it and make the most of it. It is a five-word line: "It is what it is."

Do you want proof that this phrase is now the most over-used cliché in the wide world of sports? I'll give you proof. What did Bill Belichick, coach of the New England Patriots say after his assistant coach left for the job at Notre Dame? "It is what it is. We'll deal with it." Want more? Kobe Bryant was asked about his former Lakers teammate Karl Malone and said, "It is what it is, and I want to move with the team we have here." Skip Prosser, college basketball coach at Wake Forest, when asked about his team's number one ranking earlier this year, said, "It is what it is. I can't control it." Had enough? Apparently NASCAR driver Jimmy Johnson wants the title of cliché king. When asked about finishing second in the Nextel Cup Championship, he responded with two: "We showed up and gave 110%, and it is what it is." I've got more, but I will spare you because you are probably reaching the point of cliché nausea.

So, what does "It is what it is" mean? Psychologist Dan Powell says the phrase means, "It happened. I'm going to forget about it. I'm going to move on ... There is nothing that can be done about it." Theologian Reinhold Niebuhr was probably a much deeper thinker than the aforementioned sports stars, but his Serenity Prayer has much the same line of thinking. "Lord help me to accept the things I cannot change ... " is Niebuhr's wording in the prayer. We cannot undo the past, and bad choices cannot be unmade. There are illnesses and diseases that are not going to be cured today or next month or next year. We cannot let the things that can't be changed paralyze us. We must accept some things and then move on with our lives. Hey, "it is what it is," and that's more than a cliché. It's the truth.

Your loving pastor, who always gives 110%, Steve

"Heeeere's Johnny"
I find some epitaphs to be amusing. For example, "Here lies Johnny Yeast. Pardon me for not rising." Or how about this one? "Here lies the body of Jonathan Blake. Stepped on the gas instead of the brake." There is this one from Albany, New York: "Born 1903 – Died 1942.

Looked up the elevator shaft to see if the car was on the way down. It was." And this one from a cemetery in England, "The children of Israel wanted bread and the Lord sent them manna. Old clerk Wallace wanted a wife, and the Devil sent him Anna." And my all time favorite, from a headstone somewhere in Georgia, "I told you I was sick." And now this. A syndicated gossip columnist is reporting that in her interview with Johnny Carson in 1983, he was asked what he wanted on his epitaph. His response: "I'll be right back." If only it was true. I have missed Johnny Carson since his retirement. Oh, I like Leno and Letterman, but I miss Johnny. And the King of Late Night's recent death and subsequent tributes have reminded me just how much I miss his brand of humor. For many years "the monologue" was the last thing I watched before going "beddy-bye."

The truth is, he won't be back. As someone said of life, "This ain't no dress rehearsal." We don't get to do it over. There are no mulligans. As many of you have observed, the older we get, the faster life seems to move. I mean where has it gone? I am trying more than ever to make my life count for something and to make a difference in this world. What will they say about us after we are gone?

First Baptist Church of Carrollton, Georgia
(Photograph by Holmes Photography)